Don't Need
No Soaps,
My Life Is
Soap Enough!

by Bea Joyner

To Dedra,

Whose husband made the
purchase & thanks to him
I have a new oil. Read &
Enjoy!

Bea Joyner

...DNNSMLISE

DNNSMLISE...   Bea Joyner

Published by:
Busy As A Bea Productions
PO Box 40716
Philadelphia, Pennsylvania 19107

Cover and book design by Gail Harris of ArrisHouse Designs
Photographs and poems by Beatrice Joyner
Back cover photograph by Obrafo

Copyrighted 1999
Library of Congress Catalog Number: 98-93644
ISBN: 0-9659035-2-4

Printed in the United States of America
10 9 8 7 6 5 4 3 2 1

DNNSMLISE...

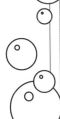

Contents

DNNSMLISE...   Bea Joyner

Part Two:
The Real Parents Training Manual Continued

Part Three:
Survival Techniques 67

DNNSMLISE...

...DNNSMLISE

DEDICATION

Thanks are due to so many but God is first on the list for all the talents, knowledge, skills and abilities that have been given to me.

Thanks to my family ...

To Grandpop William Croston Sr. who I never knew but it is his love of family that continues in me.

To my mother, Alphonsa B. Joyner, who insisted I learn how to write.

To my father, Alan E. Joyner Sr., (deceased) who insisted that nothing less than my best was good enough.

To my brothers Alan Joyner Jr., Jerry Joyner and my cousin Noel Hawkins (all deceased) for their belief in my talents but especially because they loved me as I am, not as anyone else thought I should be. Keep on loving me!

Thanks to my friends ...

To Urban Journeys Collective (Jonnetta Bagby, Kai Bey, Daveda Brown and Pamoja Payne) my photographic sisters for our commitment to promoting positive images of our communities and who taught me the importance of hugs!

To Gail Harris, my friend and sister whose talents made this book and other projects so beautiful. Thanks for being willing to listen to me read these chapters as we rode home from work and insisting I could make things funny even when I didn't think I could.

To Julianna Anderson, Jackie Bailey, Shirley Beard, Nina Bryant, Lanina Cavicchio, Dorothy Coles, Lula Cooper, Marleen Duley, Glennie Fetters, Gail Harris, (yes, I have more to tell

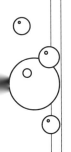

Don't Need No Soaps, My Life Is Soap Enough!

you!) Celestine Wilson-Hughes, Betty Potter, Nisa Rah, Juanita Stamps, Urban Journeys Collective, Debbie Welch, and Bobbi Willis who are constantly teaching me the meaning of friendship. You have loved and supported my works and efforts but more importantly to me, you refuse to allow me to share only my joys with you. You have each insisted that I share my sorrows as well. You sometimes have to remind me that you aren't just "anyone", you're my friends thru it all! Don't give up on teaching me, I'm still learning!

To Frank Tyson, you've been a long time and true friend. You never hesitate to push me to use all my talents and your threats to kick my butt are usually enough to get me busy! Thanks for your support, I love you dearly!

To Terri Johnson, thank you for editing this book. Terri, you swear that God sent me to you at just the right moment. If so, I'm very grateful because your gift to me was to help me organize DNNSMLISE. Thank you so much!

Thanks to those of you who have taken me through experiences both good and bad — you made me find strengths I didn't know I had.

And most importantly (after God, Mom and Pop) thanks to Jamilah and Askari for choosing me to be your mother. In raising you I became the woman I am. I am so proud of who and what you are. My prayer is that you achieve all that your talents have in store for you. Always remember to keep God first and never lose your sense of humor!

...DNNSMLISE

DNNSMLISE...   Bea Joyner

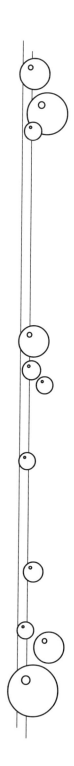

DNNSMLISE...

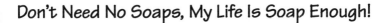

EPIGRAPH

Expansion:
*"Today I begin to expand my mind,
by appreciating myself."*

Beatrice Joyner

DNNSMLISE...   Bea Joyner

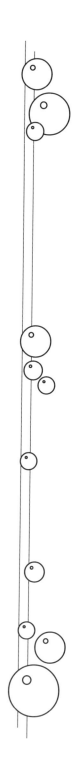

DNNSMLISE...

INTRODUCTION

This is the story of a Black female who was not on drugs, didn't prostitute for a living, or participate in any number of typically negative images that America seems to feel we must have in order for our story to be important enough to be told. It is the story of a sister who continues to struggle and survive with her sanity in tact in a world that seems hell bent on driving her insane. This book was written as a survival tactic after some particularly trying episodes of my life. As the old folks say about gas, "There's more room out, than in." If you don't release the negative energy you experience, you begin to become negative. I want none of that. I strongly believe that "God don't like ugly", so I admit to the negatives in my life and let them go.

There are many of us who defy the odds, survive and prosper. I feel our stories need to be told. We are of many hues, educational levels, and economic situations. Some of us are mothers of one or many, some choose not to be mothers. We are some of the sweetest people you would ever want to meet. We will put up with a lot and still give our all. We come in all shapes and sizes but because we aren't "model slim", we are the best kept secret around. We aren't seeking to bad mouth anyone, but we do want credit and our laurels for the things we do.

This book is being written as a warning to other sisters and brothers in the hopes that they don't make the same mistakes that I did. This book is not about male bashing but I do talk about my experiences with men. In fact, I am proud to be able to say some of the sweetest brothers in the world are my "bestest buddies". Besides, these things can happen to men or women. There are lots of stories that either of us can tell about how somebody has done us wrong. And you know what, they have!

I don't have time to sit on a couch (or lay on one in some psychiatrist's office) crying about what has happened to me. If anyone told you life is fair, they lied. Bad guys prosper and good guys lose, but it's all part of life. So you have to keep on struggling to survive. ***If it's not harder than the Middle Passage, you have no right to give up. You get 15 minutes tops for crying, after that... DEAL WITH IT!***

I have been fortunate enough that the Lord has not given me more than I could bear. Of course I have some disagreement about what I think I can bear. I sent one brother running when I started talking about challenging the Lord for what he has sent my way. I think I heard him yell something about lightning bolts and pestilence as he turned the corner. Thankfully, the Lord looks out for babies and fools and I stopped being a baby a long time ago.

You don't have to watch any soap operas, my life can outdo any soap for drama, action, and just down right stupidity. And most important of all, it's **REAL!**

DNNSMLISE...

PART ONE:
LOVE WILL MAKE
A HARD BEHIND AND A SOFT HEAD

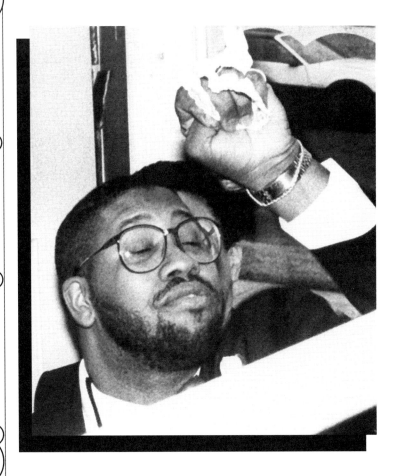

Stanley Wilson, Jr. Catches the Garter

...DNNSMLISE

DNNSMLISE...   Bea Joyner

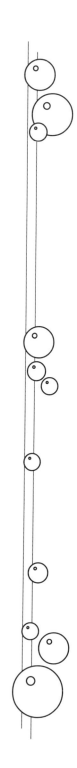

DNNSMLISE...

The Wedding and the Divorce

There was none! No wedding, no gifts, no gown! Big mistake. If I had gotten married at least I would have had the satisfaction of ripping up the wedding pictures and throwing the glasses, dishes, iron, pots, and pans when the relationship ended. Instead I have to control myself because any glasses, dishes, iron, pots or pans were bought with my own money. As I am less than well off, I can't afford to replace them. I can't even grit my teeth because I'd ground them into nubs and the dental bill would be too high for my non-existing budget.

The next big surprise was the need for a divorce. I didn't get married for a number of reasons. I hadn't seen one that made it worth the effort. I thought I could take care of myself and I didn't want the State in my business. More importantly, I really didn't think the relationship would last forever and I wanted the freedom to walk away without any ties. WRONG! The State was all in my business because I stayed "too long at the fair". It seems that Pennsylvania declares a relationship a marriage after seven years. I was with him for fourteen. You can't imagine my shock and surprise when I learned I had to get a divorce! Moral: If I am stupid enough to live with another man, (and I'm not) I'm leaving no later than six years. Besides, I've learned from my mistakes, I want a wedding so I'll have some things to throw.

There was also a real possibility that I might have had to pay spousal support. Honey, that would have been a whole 'nother volume! It took a while, but finally I was able to pay for the divorce. When I got the final decree of the divorce, there was no gold seal. I was told that the paper with the gold seal is filed with the City or the State. I don't care. All I want is my gold seal to prove I got something out of the deal. They don't

...DNNSMLISE

15

understand how much that little gold seal means to me! Remember there was no marriage license to tear up while throwing pots and pans. Without the gold seal it didn't mean as much. So what did I do? I bought a Mickey Mouse watch to celebrate. Hey, I'm easily entertained!

Love Will Make a Hard Behind and a Soft Head

I have to admit, I was deeply in love with that man. I adored him and thought he could do no wrong or if he did, I was willing to forgive him. One of my girlfriends described me as having his name etched not just on my heart, but on the inside of my eyeballs. I was unable to take a real look at what I was doing. Want an example? I tried to help him out (this was early in the separation) by allowing him to use the car that was being paid for out of my paycheck. Meanwhile, I'm struggling with two young children on the Southeastern Pennsylvania Transit Authority (SEPTA), and I was paying the car insurance as well. It took me a while before I got tired of my behind getting harder and harder while my head was getting softer and softer. I can't tell you I had a mystical experience and suddenly was awakened to the truth. It was a slow process, moment by moment. One of those moments came when I heard the song "I Can Do Bad By Myself" and realized I could do real well by myself. It took me a few years to finally leave, but when I did I knew I would not be returning. He had cured me of the fascination of being in love with a fool. I had his name sandblasted off my heart and my eyeballs and refused to have it put back. He was shocked at first when I left, but he was sure I would return. He thought if he showed me a little patience, I would probably come back to my senses.

Don't Need No Soaps, My Life Is Soap Enough!

I have a tendency to believe people, especially someone I loved so deeply. A friend of mine described it as being so in love that when that person tells you its sunny outside, you believe them, even though it's raining like cats and dogs. I got tired of catching colds and damn near dying of pneumonia before I realized something was wrong with this picture. That's when I moved me and my kids into to my own place. And you know what I discovered - I could do real well by myself. There's something to be said about being able to come home, close and lock your door knowing no one else is coming in behind you. The most important lesson I learned is to value my peace of mind. Believe me, it won't get sold cheaply again.

...DNNSMLISE

DNNSMLISE...   Bea Joyner

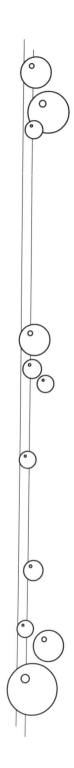

DNNSMLISE...

PART TWO:
THE REAL PARENTS TRAINING MANUAL

Kids and Bears and Bears and Kids
Jamilah & Askari

...DNNSMLISE

DNNSMLISE...   Bea Joyner

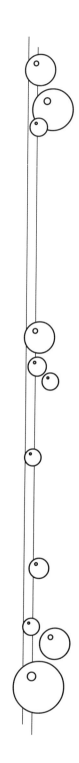

DNNSMLISE...

Why Women Sleep So Much During Pregnancy and Other Related Mysteries of Life

Okay, I'll give you your first introduction to the Real Parents Training Manual. Why do pregnant women sleep so much? And why am I even bothering to explore this topic? Well, for one thing, it was the other related mysteries that interested me but it seems it begins with the pregnancy. Everyone knows women sleep tremendous amounts of time while they are pregnant, it is expected. In some instances the man seems to get as much sleep as the woman does. This is because the body is preparing itself for what it knows is coming. What is coming is this will be the last time in the next eighteen, nineteen or twenty years that you will be able to sleep without having to attend to someone else's needs before your own.

For many of us, the first few weeks of a baby's life is our first introduction to sleep deprivation. This is not the same as staying out all night long partying and having fun. This is real, laboratory style, strap them to the bed torture. It may also be the first time you question your sanity for deciding to become a parent. If you can get two straight hours of sleep, you think you have died and gone to heaven. Why? Because by the time the baby wakes up, you feed and change him or her and get them back to sleep, you have fifty million things to do to get ready for the next round. It is very early in this process that some parents find themselves ready to lay down to catch some sleep and are shocked to find the baby is ready to be fed and changed again! You have to understand that the problem is the parents have worked through their last sleeping period while the baby got theirs. That's why you will hear new parents talk about sleeping when the baby sleeps, they have to. It's the only time you will get any rest.

And to make matters worse, people get on your case for sleeping so much. Sometimes it's the first sign that you are pregnant. People will tell you, "Girl, you're sleeping an awful lot these days. Are you sure you aren't pregnant? Or "You're going to sleep you life away." Or the ever popular, "I don't remember sleeping that much with any of my three, four or five children. What's wrong with you?" There is nothing wrong with you. Mother Nature is just trying to help you out by making you tired enough to the point that you admit you have to go to sleep before you keel over.

Obviously if you can get the baby to sleep through the night, you can get more sleep. Everyone will tell you the child can't sleep through the night because they are hungry. I thought I would solve that problem by following the advice of my mother and mother-in-law of putting cereal in Jamilah's bottle. I started with a little, it didn't work. I added more, same results. Finally I put so much cereal in Jamilah's baby bottle that the gruel was gray looking and so thick, I had to cut a hole in the nipple that was at least a half inch wide to allow it to pass out. Did it work? Of course not! That's when I learned that Jamilah was determined to be a night owl. I think she would have volunteered to help me with Askari when he was a baby in the middle of the night because it gave her an excuse to be up! And I'm having flashback of those days because Jamilah is now a night owl again at college. She wants to come home, keep her same hours of staying up all night long and can't understand why I demand she goes to bed. It's memories of sleep depravation!

This sleep deprivation flows and ebbs like the tide. Once you manage to get the baby to sleep through the night, you will find a period of maybe a year and a half of being able to get

DNNSMLISE...

Don't Need No Soaps, My Life Is Soap Enough!

some rest. After all Mother Nature is not out to destroy mankind, she has to let us get some sleep. Then the next phase begins called potty training and bed wetting. In order to train your child, you have to catch both daytime and nighttime wetting before you can declare the child free of diapers. So now you have to learn their physical body functions all over again so you can wake the child once, twice, sometimes three times during the night to drag them to the potty. There you stand in a daze with a dazed child who now begins to formulate in their mind that you are a child abuser for dragging them out of a perfectly good sleep to sit their behind on a cold toilet seat. Of course you have to make the same proud parent noise of joy and happiness when they wet in the toilet like you do during the day when you are wide awake. Of course this doesn't change the child's mind that you are a child abuser because you sat their little warm behind on the dreaded seat. The seat may be that great big opening that stands high above their head, that can only be reached with your assistance. If not, it's one of those cute musical numbers that allows you to catch some sleep while leaning on the wall until it chimes. That's when you notice the child is asleep, had no intention of wetting at that moment and is just hoping the authorities show up to arrest you and return them to their nice warm bed.

Later in life the sleep deprivation returns when your son or daughter has learned to drive your car and wants to stay out all night. Suddenly you find yourself unable to sleep until the car and your child has returned home safely. It's amazing how every little sound or accident report can guarantee you won't sleep for another hour or two when it's already two in the morning and you have to get up at six. Curfew does not seem to make an impression on your child once they get behind the wheel. Especially if they've been away to college. I had heard parents say their child has to be in when it's time for the parent to go to

...DNNSMLISE

bed. I know I have become such a light sleeper, that I need to know Jamilah is in the bed so I can get some sleep.

And is it necessary to refer to pregnancy as a "Bun in the oven?" I understand that the expression came about because there is something inside the woman that is growing and will eventually come out. I think it's mainly because women go through sweats at the oddest of times. It's a preview of the same sweats that come later during menopause. Only by that time nobody has sympathy for you like they did when you were pregnant. You find yourself making everyone at home freeze while your are trying to regulate your body heat. That body heat is being produced because you're trying to get the last egg out of your body in the process known as menopause. Once again your hormones are creating havoc in your body as you shift into another phase of life. Only people don't care or make a fuss over you the way they do when you had that bun in the oven. They just want you to get over your insanity as quickly as possible so you can take care of them just like you used to. *Ha!* What they don't realize is that menopause also leaves you with the realization that they are now old enough to take care of themselves without any assistance from you. That's why they try to tell you you're insane, you're waking up to that fact. Well, some of us don't wake up till then. Me, I knew it all along. My children will need to be in the comfort of their own homes so that I won't have to freeze them out because I'm having hot flashes. We can remain a wholesome, loving family but only if we have separate households.

Well, if you haven't been involved in these things, you don't have a clue what I'm talking about. If you have, you know I'm right about the necessarily of keeping that Real Parent's Training Manual away from us. If we knew all this at the beginning of the process, who among us would want to bother?!!

DNNSMLISE...

Rise and Shine, Mom is Packing a Water Bottle

When I first became a single parent, one of the hardest things for me was getting my children up and ready for school by myself. For some reason that I don't fully understand, children respond better to a male voice at times like these. My children wanted to be the living dead when I needed them to get up and get dressed. I had tried everything to get them up. I was gentle, I pleaded, I screamed, I dumped them out of the bed, and yes, I even beat them. I gave them their own clock and talked to them about the importance of being on time. I tried to treat them like children. I tried treating them like adults. Nothing seemed to work.

Finally, I found the perfect solution - a water bottle. I don't even remember how I discovered it. I would call them... no response. I would warn them... no response. Then I sprayed them. Suddenly, they were doing the dance of life as they leaped from their bed as that cold stream of water hit them. Hey, whatever works!

Dead, Dying or Bleeding

The other problem I had with getting my children up in the morning was their constant fighting. I seemed to fail to remember my own childhood fights with my sister. Only the more pleasant memories seem to survive. Besides I'm sure I never gave my mother that much trouble. I was too scared of her to want to cross her path. I saw how she beat my brothers and sisters and believe me, I didn't want that lady on my tail. I wasn't about to give my mother a hard way to go! But she was no different than most of the mothers in our neighborhood. I remember seeing kids who defied their mothers' authority. I was sure they were on a kamikaze mission. One mother even wrote down in a book everything her son did to deserve a beating. When she finally got to him, she had the book in hand to remind her just in case she had forgot any offense. I am well aware that most of our parents would be arrested for child abuse these days for this type of behavior. For most of us, our parents weren't trying to abuse us, they were simply doing what they felt was best for us. It did hurt them more than it did us because it is hard to constantly discipline your children. And you know what, most of us turned out pretty well.

I know now why they don't pass out the real parents' manual when folks are thinking about having children. No one would do it if they had been told the truth! Of course, no one told me that children have to fight in the morning like they have to breath. It's a natural order of business. My problem is I don't have time for it.

One morning while I was trying to get my children dressed, fed and out of the house, I found myself speaking in "Parent Tongues". Once again the plot to drive mommy crazy was in full effect. I had gotten them dressed and sat them at the table to eat while I got washed and dressed. Suddenly they burst into the bathroom while I was showering screaming and yelling — accusing each other of having committed some dastardly deed. My eyes turned into flame throwers but it's hard to keep the flame going while you have water in them. I could feel an energy coming over me and before I knew it, I was speaking in my parents' voice. I was able to maintain some of myself so the words were my own. I yelled *"Unless you are dead, dying, or bleeding, get out!"*

Don't Need No Soaps, My Life Is Soap Enough!

You have to understand, I had promised myself I would never do some of the things to my children that my parents did to me. However, the longer I am a parent, the more I realize the wisdom of what my parents did. Every parent has sayings. I think it is the brain's way of preventing us from having strokes by putting us into "Autoparent". Some of the things we say are truly in "Parent Tongues" but our children understand us as well as we understood them as babies, when all they could speak was grunts and groans. I remember my parents had a hard time remembering our names. I thought that was terrible to confuse me with my siblings. I know now it's understandable since they had nine children. We were lucky they didn't get amnesia and forget us all together. I have a hard time with just two names when I'm really upset.

The meaning of what I yelled at my children is not hard to understand, it just doesn't make much sense unless you have two whirling tornadoes in your bathroom while you are trying to get washed and dressed in the fifteen minutes they have left you after getting them ready. But for those of you who have no concept of what I'm saying, I'll explain. Unless my children had killed themselves (or each other), or were seriously injured, they were to stay out of my way until I had had a chance to get ready. It was my way of saying, "Unless you want to die this morning, stay at that table, eat your breakfast and be ready when I come out of my room!" Dead, dying or bleeding is quicker and more direct when you're in "Autoparent".

There is one other saying that has become a favorite of mine. When someone asks how old my children are I say "If I let them live, they'll be (blank) age!" I can say this because I'm not quite into "Autoparent" and I don't need to speak in tongues!

Chewing Cream of Wheat

The other difficulty with mornings was trying to get my children to eat a good healthy breakfast. They don't seem to understand that there are millions of other children who would be glad to have their mother rant and rave about the value of a good meal in the morning while providing it. But what do they know.

One morning I was fixing a breakfast of eggs and sausage. Understand you're talking to a single parent trying to get two children out of the house who would feel it is their life's duty to drive mom crazy. Askari was about three at the time. He wandered into the kitchen to ask what was for breakfast. When I told him, he said "Yuck". I asked him to repeat it and he did. I said "Boy, one morning about ten years from now, you'll be begging me to fix you some eggs." Well he's almost thirteen and it hasn't happen yet. What do I know?

Before my children were old enough to fix their own breakfast the struggle to get them to eat was fierce. I finally decided to try Cream of Wheat. Now I remember well the mornings my mother fixed Cream of Wheat for us. I still get choked up on the memory of some of the championship size lumps. I was determined that I would never serve my kids lumpy cereal. This particular morning, I had made a prize winning bowl of very smooth Cream of Wheat. I sat my children down to the table with instructions to eat quickly while I showered and dressed. Mind you, I know my children are small eaters so I didn't fix large portions. Twenty to thirty minutes passed, and my children are still sitting there with that same bowl of cereal. "Why haven't you finished?", I asked. "We can't swallow it.", they informed me very calmly. In disbelief, I watched two children

Don't Need No Soaps, My Life Is Soap Enough!

Chew Cream of Wheat. "You don't have to chew it, you swallow it!", I yelled. They began to cry in unison, "It hurts my throat!"

By now my eyes are flame throwers. This is from two children who practically swallow Dorito Corn Chips (their favorite food at this time) *Whole*! It's times like these that I am sure the plot to drive me crazy is in full force. I poured enough milk into their bowls that they needed a straw to drink it. They took one look at my face and somehow those bowls of cereal disappeared. I have no idea if they chewed it or swallowed it that morning. I had a hard time seeing around the flames.

Growing Moldy Sandwiches Under the Bed

My problems of getting my children to eat continued with preparing lunches for them. I tried to do things with them my parents couldn't afford to do with us as they were trying to make ends meet while feeding nine children. I gave them choices of what they could take. The school didn't supply lunches so it had to come from home. I allowed them to pick out their own lunch meat and I didn't force wheat bread on them. It didn't help.

One day I noticed a strange odor coming from my children's room. It was not pleasant! I cleaned the room, made sure the laundry was done, but still the smell continued. They were not allowed to eat in their room so I was baffled by the smell. Finally, I looked under the dresser and found an amazing science project growing there. Someone, (of course no one would claim credit for it) had placed or thrown a sandwich under the dresser. The variety of mold was a wonder to see, white, yellow, green, black and runny!

...DNNSMLISE

DNNSMLISE...   Bea Joyner

Now, they could just as easily have thrown them away or traded them in school and I would never have known the difference. I do understand about having to eat food you don't want. I know some parents force kids to eat unbelievable meals. I remember my mother's pigtails and black-eyed peas and my father's fish roe. To this day, there are certain foods I won't touch because I was forced to eat them when I was unable to resist without someone writing out my death certificate. I don't care how much luck black-eyed peas are suppose to bring, I won't eat them!

I remember the tactics we went through to get rid of food we didn't like. I remember fighting to sit near the legs of the kitchen table. We discovered the legs were hollow and many a green pea found its way to its abyss. Mom must have suspected something because the table got changed. If we asked to go to the bathroom during a meal, my mother would inspect our pockets before we could leave.

One of my aunts had it down to a science. We were sent to spend some time with her for a vacation (as a break for my mother). If she fixed something we didn't like, we would refuse to eat it. She never fussed and we were dismissed from the table. *However*, when we came looking for our next meal, there was that item back on our plate. Sometimes we would play around with it looking for sympathy from her. We didn't have to eat it but you got mighty hungry. I don't know who holds the record for the longest hold out but we quickly learned that just because she didn't have children of her own didn't mean she didn't know how to handle other people's children. Oh, I forgot to mention, she was a school teacher. Boy, I was glad I was never in her class!

Actually, I probably should be glad my kids conduct science projects under their dresser. I'm worried as to what happens

DNNSMLISE...

when they get smart enough to figure out how they're being caught!

One Mouse and the Fish Committed Suicide

My children wanted to have a cat or a dog but we couldn't because we live in an apartment. They decided they wanted a box turtle. I went to the pet store to get one but the salesman told me they were illegal in the state of Pennsylvania because too many children had gotten salmonella poisoning from putting them up to their mouths. I explained my situation to the salesman and asked if he could recommend another pet. He said "How about an iguana?" I had these visions of Godzilla movies. I thought maybe I misunderstood him so I asked to see one. He showed it to me and I was right, there was a miniature Godzilla in the cage. He told me how they make good pets, etc., etc. I asked if he could recommend anything else. He said "How about a chameleon?" (I figured it out later that either he had a fascination for lizards or they had a few they needed to unload.) I had visions of something assuming my shape and size and taking over my household. Finally I asked him what do they eat. The iguana eats fruits and vegetables. The chameleon eats milliworms which I had never heard of. I asked how many do they eat and how do you buy them. He told me they eat a few at a time and you can refrigerate the rest. I had no intention of giving my refrigerator over to some worms. Needless to say there are no lizards of any kind in my house, especially since he told me they grow to the size of their cage and live long.

...DNNSMLISE

DNNSMLISE...   Bea Joyner

A few years later (still petless) my daughter went away to camp. When I went to pick her up, she begged and pleaded with me to let her bring home two small white mice. I knew how much they both wanted a pet so I reluctantly agreed. We bought a small plastic cage, food and bedding. The smallest mouse died shortly after she got them home. She named the other one Fergus, after a friend. I think Fergus let the other one know the cage wasn't big enough for two mice and he did him in.

By now the children were into a visitation schedule of every other week-end with their father. This meant I would have to feed and change the water. I quickly figured out Fergus would survive for three days without my doing anything. I just made sure they changed the bedding, fed and watered him before they left. I wasn't ready for a long term relationship with a rodent either. Friends assured me the mice wouldn't live long. They were right about the one, but good old Fergus lasted for two years before he kicked the bucket!

During one of their visits with their father, my children got gold fish. You know the kind that you win at amusement parks and come in a little plastic bag. Well I hit the ceiling. I was not taking on the responsibility of another mouth to feed in my house that couldn't pay for its own upkeep. They wanted the fish so bad that they set out water for it at their father's. You can't put them directly in City water, the chemicals would kill them. They then went back after school, packed up the water and the fish and brought them home. Of course there was no fish food. I told them to get it from their father, I wasn't taking on another bill. They began feeding the fish bread.

With Fergus gone, they used his cage for the new pets. There was no filtering system so they began setting out buckets of water in the hallway so they could change it every two to three days. I had visions of the water getting spilled all over the carpeting. I gave them 4 - 6 large soda bottles so they could set out

DNNSMLISE...

the water. I had washed them out and they told me the water would kill the fish. They were talking about the few drops that were left inside the bottle. I think they took one look at my face and decided the fish would survive but they wouldn't if they didn't take those bottles. Again friends told me the fish would die in a few days. They lived for three months.

When Jamilah went to camp again, Askari had to take care of the fish. He told me one day it was a "two people job" and he should have made her take them to camp with her. When she returned, I told her it was her turn to change the water. Askari had earned some money so he wanted me to take them to get the food. I told her to change the water while I was at work and I'd take them for the food when I got back. I called them when I was ready to leave work and told them to be ready to go as soon as I came in. I was told they didn't need it because the fish had died. When I asked how, I was told they jumped out. I was mystified. They had been in the same container all this time, why should they jump out now?

When I got home, I asked Jamilah what happened. She told me she had put them in a smaller container so she could change the water. For some reason and logic known only to her, she went and took a nap. She said she found them later, one was all curled up and the other was bright orange. Unfortunately, Askari could not see the humor in it and ran out of the room crying. I went to comfort him and God knows why, I've agreed to get another pet — you guessed it — a mouse or a fish!

My Daughter Gets a Job

One day when Jamilah was sixteen years old, she came to me very excited about having found a job. She had searched the want ads and was accepted for a

...DNNSMLISE

telemarketing position. I tried to tell her what she was in for but she started yelling "I can make $500 a week!" I advised her to ask the company what the average salary is for most employees but she tried to accuse me of interfering and not wanting her to have a job. I asked her about her grades as we have been battling over them for the last three years but she assured me she could keep up. Her hours were from 5:00 P.M. to 9:00 P.M. The most I could get her to do was to listen to one of my friends whom she knows and respects about her experiences with a telemarketing position. Remember love isn't the only thing that will make a hard behind and a soft head. Greed will do it too!

I picked Jamilah up after her first night of work. She had gotten two successful phone calls where the people accepted her product. The job entailed offering people a free medical exam from a chiropractic doctor's office. She said she would be paid $5 for each call that was accepted after the first two. I was worried and concerned that she would only get $10 for the four hours of work. I had to keep asking her about her salary before she finally told me she would get $5 a hour (minimum wage). I tried to warn her again but she still was sure she could do it. The next night she decided she wasn't up to going to work because she had had "a rough day in school." It was only because she hadn't gotten her working papers which were required that I didn't force her to go.

The following night she did work as she had the working papers. When I picked her up, the first thing out of her mouth was, **"I Quit!"** I said "Oh, no Girl Friend, you've got $500 to make." She rolled her eyes as I started laughing. She said, "It's not funny! I'm tired of people hanging up on me." I tried to explain again how hard that kind of work is, how everyone is not cut out to do it but some people can be quite successful at it. It didn't help that I had tears rolling down my face from laughing.

DNNSMLISE...

Don't Need No Soaps, My Life Is Soap Enough!

She told me how one woman had fifteen calls. She tried to ask her how she did it. The woman told her she followed the script they had given her. "Girl Friend" said she had tried that but it didn't help. She said one man had told her, "Nothing is for free!" as he hung up. I told her it was a good thing she hadn't called me. She agreed saying "I know you would have hung up!" I tried to show her the good points of her experiences. She would have been stronger from having dealt with disagreeable people, she would have been better able to deal with rejection. Of course I had to go back through my speech about "Welcome to the real world" and how life is hard. I asked her what would she have done if she had to deal with that job or be out on the street (from lack of money) in weather like the severe winter we had just survived. She agreed she probably would have had to keep trying.

The next morning as I was getting dressed, I heard an announcement on the radio that one T.V. station was going to broadcast a report about a telemarketing scam of a company that was offering a free medical exam. The company would inquire if the person had medical coverage and use that information to file claims in the person's name. Of course you know I had to tell "Girl Friend". All she could do was grin and tell me she was going in that day, show them her working papers and quit. She said it was also out of concern for me because she didn't want anyone suing me because she had worked there and was a minor. As Barry White says, "Sure you're right!"

...DNNSMLISE

My Son - "Slick Rick"

Have you noticed that the name you gave your child at birth is not always the one that remains with them for their life time? I think it's because their real attributes and personality come out later. Take Askari. His new name is "Slick Rick", as I have a hustler in the making. If you're not careful, he can talk, whine or beg his way out of many things. I have to be constantly on my guard.

When Askari was in kindergarten, he came to me one day and said he needed some money. "For what?", I asked. Jamilah yelled out "He wants to buy his girl friend some jewelry!" I politely told him when he was ready to buy jewelry for his girl friend, he would use his own money and not mine. Then I asked the important question, who was she? It turns out it was a first grader. I mean the kid wasn't even in real school yet and here he was trying to buy gifts for girls!

He recently came home with a spelling test paper with a score of ninety. I congratulated him and began to encourage him to get a hundred next time. He started grinning and said "Nope, next time I'll get a ninety-five and the time after that, a hundred." Now I know Askari is capable of getting a hundred on a spelling test so I asked him why wouldn't he do so. He grinned and said "Because if I don't and wait two more tests, I can get a homework pass. (A homework pass allows you not to do homework for a day.) He had figured out how to beat the grading system at school by not getting a hundred right away. Three improvements were worth more. Of course I had to tell his teacher. As soon as I started explaining, he understood. "Slick Rick".

Askari was off from school one day so Daveda Brown agreed to keep him part of the day. He was 9 or ten at the time. I told

Don't Need No Soaps, My Life Is Soap Enough!

him to take a couple of videos with him to keep him occupied. When I called Daveda later to check on him, she had a question. She wanted to know if I allowed Askari to watch "Blazing Saddles". I said no, it's rated "R" and I don't allow him or Jamilah to watch "R" rated movies. "Slick Rick" strikes again! He knows I bought the video for me and I forgot to check his bag to see what video he had chosen. He told Daveda when she questioned him about it, "I've watched it before." Of course he said it very innocently while batting his baby browns. You have to watch out for that, he bats them very well! Yes, he had watched it before but without my permission. When he came home, he wanted to know why he couldn't watch the video. I told him because it was rated "R" and I don't allow him to watch them.

Later on he started singing the "I'm Tired" song from the movie. The character that sings the song is mimicking Marlena Dietrich as a "hussy". That would be all I needed. I could envision getting a call from the nuns at his school about him singing the song. Actually, I guess it's not half as bad or graphic as some of the songs on the radio these days but I don't want to have to explain them either.

Here We Go to the GYN

As if I needed more material to add to this book! I have known since the day I gave birth to Jamilah, that some day she would become a sexually active female. However, according to my game plan that was not supposed to happen until she was twenty-five and married. Little did it matter that I didn't wait that long, I needed to be able to keep my sanity. I remember the day she came to me at age eight to tell me she was having stomach cramps. I quickly told her to get on the floor and do some sit-ups. When that didn't work, I took her to the doctor. He reassured me that she wasn't menstruating but would probably begin around age ten. As sweat poured down my face, I calmly announced, "Let's just lock up all the dogs (males) now!" I had observed men in their thirties checking out young girls who they had to know were only twelve and thirteen. I figured if we locked these kinds of dogs up, I wouldn't have to go to jail for them trying to get to Jamilah. It did help that Jamilah didn't start menstruating until much later than ten years old.

One day Jamilah told me she was having problems with her period. She hadn't had a period in two months but now it was on and her flow was heavy. We agreed that we should probably make an appointment with a gynecologist (GYN). Later that morning she called me to say she had passed a large mass. She said she felt fine and wasn't having any pain. I told her I would call my doctor and see what he said. The nurse at his office said it was probably best to have her examined right away as it was possible that she had had a miscarriage. Well that's when the panic button was jammed straight through the wall! I didn't think she was sexually active let alone pregnant. I know many women have gone through this and are now proud grandmothers. "Nana" or "Mom Mom" is not something I'm looking forward to being called until both of my kids have finished college.

I told the nurse I would bring her in right away as one of the female doctors on staff could see her if I could get her there in the next hour or two. I called Jamilah's school to have her released. The doctor's office is close to my job. She could make the trip to me in approximately 15 minutes by the subway as opposed to me going to pick up my car, drive to the school, go to the doctor's office, look for a parking space, well, you get the idea. Unfortunately, the school didn't. I had to talk to the counselor, the nurse, the vice principal, the principal and still they said they couldn't let her go. Finally I called back to the doctor's office and spoke to the nurse. She was concerned that I calm down before I had a stroke. She agreed to call the school and they gave her a hard way to go. I called the school and told them I'd be there in twenty minutes to pick up Jamilah. I was, and I did.

Jamilah and I got to the doctor's office in short order. I was able to calm down some after I asked her if she was sexually active and she said no. I accepted that but I knew I wouldn't be satisfied until the doctor said so. The doctor said she was fine, not sexually active and Jamilah was to call her on Monday to let her know if everything was fine. I told Jamilah as we left the office, "When you become sexually active, please let me know so I don't panic." Jamilah said "Mommy, I won't tell you because you would panic." She's probably right.

Home Entertainment

My children and I are movie buffs. We'll watch the coming attractions to decide what we'll go to see next. I refuse to let them see a "R" rated movie with one or two exceptions - "Glory" and "Malcolm X" Those were must sees. However, we don't always agree on what to see. Jamilah dragged me to see "The Pet Detective." Not my kind of movie. We also rent movies from the public library. They're for free and you can keep them for a week. I've been able to introduce them to some great old movies. Askari loves comedy and I've introduced him to the Marx Brothers, Charlie Chaplain, W.C. Fields, and Laurel and Hardy. I did make the mistake of bringing home a Monty Python movie that contained too much adult

...DNNSMLISE

material for Askari to see. Fortunately Jamilah was monitoring him for me and turned it off. However, she watched it and every once in awhile, she'll break out with the "Lumberjack Song". It gives us a chance to relax and share some fun times.

We also play cards - UNO and Five Hundred are big at our house. Of course you have to be careful with my children, they will cheat. "Slick Rick" only likes to play when he's winning. If he's lost the round, he'll grab his cards quick and try to stuff them back in the deck before you can count the points. Jamilah likes to play Five Hundred not Gin Rummy because you can't do three of a kind in Gin Rummy. It requires more strategy to play it and both of them are after the quick kill. Especially if it means they can get me.

I've introduced them to dominoes which they enjoy. We have a double twelve set so it can get complicated. I bought them a game called Jenga which is a game where you stack up the wooden pieces with the object being to pull one piece from the stack without the stack falling down. "Slick Rick" is pretty good at it because he keeps practicing but keep your eye on him. He tries to hold the stack which is not allowed. He is also good at doing puzzles. I buy the 1000-pieces puzzles to keep challenging him. He and I usually do them together. He has a good eye for the spatial concepts needed to put them together. I'll be struggling to find and fit a particular piece. He'll come along and within seconds he's found it and put it in place. So now I know to hold on to the pieces I really want to fit and not let him see them.

One day the cleaning bug got a hold of my children and they not only cleaned their room but they cleaned out their closet too. They "discovered" their Scrabble and Monopoly game sets as well as a game based on trivial information. They even decided to put the cards for the trivial pursuit in order! (Don't ask me, I'm still trying to figure out how to keep that bug

DNNSMLISE...

around!) I started asking them some questions from the game but I had to stop because their frustration level was very low that day. The question that did it for them was "How many toes on a four-toe sloth?" "Four", they quickly said, pleased that they finally had a right answer. "Sixteen", I said. When they realized why, (four legs times four toes equals sixteen) I was banned from the cards. Hcy, home entertainment can only go so far.

Warning to Parents of Adolescents:
Beware the Invasion of the Body Snatchers

This is yet another chapter from the Real Parent's Training Manual. It is one of the most closely guarded secrets of parenting. Should it have been revealed sooner, human existence as we know it would have ceased to exist. Hmm, I wonder if that would be so bad.

Okay, here it is. When your children reach the ages between 11 and 13, they will leave and be replaced with a total stranger. It will look like your child. You will be lulled into believing it is your child UNTIL that monster jumps you one day. At this point, their bodies are battling an increase in hormones that will lead to adulthood but they become ranting, raving lunatics. Some become sullen and withdrawn. Others become snappish. Others in the deepest thralls will become "B&B's" (Bitc—s and Bas——s). It is during this point that you will earn, strand by strand, your gray hair. Some of you will experience ulcers and high blood pressure. You will quickly discover "Autoparent", "Flame Throwing Eyes" and "Parent Tongues" are no longer effective. I think the hormones grow them flame retardant bodies. They will make you doubt your sanity and your rationale for having decided to become a parent. I took a

...DNNSMLISE

course in parenting adolescents long before Jamilah reached that age to be prepared. It didn't help much because she didn't take the same course and refused to follow the game plan.

It doesn't help that others will tell you, "This too shall pass." People who haven't seen Jamilah for a long period of time will comment on how nicely she has grown and say how quickly the years have passed. I let them know the years did not pass quickly for me because I had to live with her. I felt each gray hair as it popped out and grew longer and longer.

The only thing you will have to show for this period of their life is:

1. *Additional bills - "I can't wear that." or "I can't wear my hair like that."*
2. *A different diet - "I only want to eat that." OR*
3. *A very strong desire to be placed in suspended animation until they reach age twenty-one when they are (HA!) legally responsible for themselves. I tried that, but they discovered the location of my cocoon. I didn't get far enough, fast enough.*

Remember the gold seal I wanted on my divorce papers, you don't get that either. I have decided to give myself "Motherhood Badges" like in the Girl Scouts. I earned my first one when I went on a daycare trip with twenty-five screaming children ages two to five. I earned two more when my children were finally through the Terrible Two's and Three's.

These activities are nothing compared to what you will go through when they become teenagers. Okay, one example. Jamilah, who had always been an "A/B" student dropped to "C/D" and felt that there was nothing wrong with that. You have to understand, I am preparing my children to be independent and self reliant. They need good grades to get into a good college, then to get a good job and then move out of my house. I tried no T.V., no phone, no trips with friends. She got indignant when

Don't Need No Soaps, My Life Is Soap Enough!

I was going to get her a tutor after she failed Geometry. When she came back two days later with a 95 on a test, I swear I grew a gray hair five feet long. Somehow, I lost it. I had plans of weaving it into a hangman's noose for her or for me when I couldn't take it any more. She finally came to her senses when her school threatened to kick her out and I said no prom.

Be forewarned that whatever experience or battle plans you think you've got as an arsenal from the first one will not work on the second one. They will be about as effective as those "Flame Throwing Eyes". I think the older ones pass your secret weapons on by osmosis. I can already see glimpses of Askari fading out and that stranger coming into focus. He has had two toothbrushes in the bathroom for two years. When I asked what the second one is for, he grinned, picked it up and began brushing his eye brows. Then I remembered his comments about how he and "his boys", 5th graders, were going after the eighth grade girls. Now I know times have changed, but I can't imagine a thirteen year old girl being interested in a eight year old boy except as practice before she moves on to her real target! That's when it becomes necessary to have a talk with her parents!

The worst part of all this is, unless you have been able to produce all of your children at the same time, this process will be repeated. Can you imagine all of your children going through this at the same time. It would be like being trapped in "Gremlins I & 2" for eight to ten years! (Some take longer to get through it than others.) Now do you understand why I said it might not be a bad idea to change man's existence as we know it. That's it! That's the key - it's a man's fault. Remember screaming that after twenty hours of hard labor. Oh, I apologize, I promised no male bashing.

Quick, for your own safety, *run for the hills for the secret location of your suspended animation chamber! It's your only hope of surviving with your sanity in tact!*

...DNNSMLISE

Have Your Children Started Speaking
a Second Language Yet?

This is another question from the "Real Training Manual on Parenting." The language I'm referring to is the "Teenage Mumbles". It creeps up on you with no warning. I noticed it when I would introduce my children to someone. When Jamilah was 2 or 3, she would take over the conversation, speaking very clearly and captivate her audience. Now both she and Askari start with that second language and I can barely understand what they are saying even when they say their names! The truth of the matter is, they have probably been mumbling for a long time but I didn't realize how pervasive it was. I've found myself repeating questions wondering if I was speaking clearly enough. I now know I was. I now know they could hear me. I now know it's that second language.

And it's amazing how quickly they can slip between the two languages. Just let them want something. Suddenly they are speaking crystal clear and they will enunciate with competition level clarity. "Mother, may I please have $5?" "Mother, may I please go over so-and-so's house?" Your first clue is the word "Mother". Usually we're "Mom, Ma, or Mommy". When my children use the word "mother", I check their foreheads to see if they have a fever and look into their eyes to see who is this stranger calling me "mother". However, as soon as your answer is in the negative, a transformation takes place.

In my household, I actually have two dialects of the second language. Jamilah speaks "Mumbles" and Askari speaks "Whining". It gets rough when they both decide to speak their second language at the same time. I think part of the problem is we were never allowed to speak in "Mumbles". The only way we would have spoken in "Mumbles" to our parents was in our dreams, or if we had decided life was no longer worth living, prepared our will and made our peace with our Maker. Our parents meant it when they said, "I brought you into this world and I'll take you out of it!" Nowadays people tell me if Mumbles is all you have to deal with, you're not doing too badly. Well, I'm sorry. I don't buy that. I can't stand children mumbling under their breath or the sucking of teeth when I'm talking to them.

Jamilah has pretty much gotten through this stage. Now when she starts to mumble, I call her Mutley. Mutley is a cartoon dog, who is a side kick to Dastardly, a bad guy. Everytime Dastardly orders Mutley to do something, Mutley mumbles under his breath. I've shown Jamilah that cartoon. For some reason, she doesn't think it is a very complimentary nickname. But hey, she doesn't mumble as much any more. Now if I could just prevent Askari from using that second language...!!!

Girl Friends Warn Me I'm Suffering From Delusions That My Children Will Leave Home

I look at my friends who have grown children and many of them are still home. I thought kids are supposed to grow up, go away to college or get a full time job, and move out. That's when my life begins again. I'll be a person instead of "That's Jamilah and Askari's mother." I strongly believe that all children should leave home after a certain age and only return for visits — brief ones. My girlfriends and some male friends have told me I'm dreaming or suffering from delusions. I don't care. It worked in "Peter Pan." I'm going to keep saying "I do believe, I do believe!"

...DNNSMLISE

DNNSMLISE...   Bea Joyner

I can tell you when my so called delusions began. I hear a career military man say how he had been telling his sons since they were four, "Eighteen and out." They were following his advice as his oldest son (who had just turned eighteen) was leaving in a few months for the service. I thought I'd better get busy as Askari was eight at the time so I was behind schedule. I don't think I'll have any problem getting Jamilah to leave home. We are too much alike and constantly bump heads. I think she's counting not just the months until she leaves but the days and hours.

I waited for the right moment to bring up the subject with Askari. We were walking to the bus one day and his nose was running. I asked him where were his tissues, he told me I should have them. Perfect timing I thought to talk to him about being responsible for himself. I told him I was preparing him to be able to take care of himself, that he would one day be on his own. I told him he didn't want to be depending on some female he didn't even like, just to take care of him. "And by the way", I said, "Eighteen and out." He looked at me and grinned and said "Twenty-five and out." I said "Let me explain this to you. I have no intention of washing your clothes and cooking your meals for the rest of my life. And I'm not putting up with funky socks and late nights. Eighteen and out!"

Askari decided to change tactics. He looked at me and said "I'll get a maid." He was grinning just a little too hard for me so I asked "A maid for me?" "No," he said. "A maid for my room." I asked, "What's her name?" I had a real strong suspicion that her name was Bea. He wisely didn't answer. I said "Let me explain this to you. You have to be the boss to pay the cost. There will be no live-in and one more time, eighteen and out." He grinned and said "Forty and out." Now I have seen too many people still living at home in their thirties who have never really lived away from home. I have every intention of not only be-

DNNSMLISE...

Don't Need No Soaps, My Life Is Soap Enough!

coming a person again, but also a woman free to come and go as I please without worrying about anyone waiting on me to come home to cook and clean. I won't be able to do that as easily with children at home.

I remember very clearly how my mother pushed me out of the nest. She charged me a substantial rent and I had a curfew. I quickly figured out that I could pay rent elsewhere and have no curfew. I got the hint. I think many parents are making it too easy for their children to remain at home. The lights come on when they throw the switch and the heat comes on when it gets cold without any effort on their part. I understand that times are hard and the economics are difficult. What worries me is I don't think these kids are learning the survival skills they will need to deal with life. It's best to learn these skills while you're young and your body can adjust to being cold and hungry if necessary. You don't get to eat steak when all you can afford is hot dogs. If you spent your money on a fine car and you have no place to live, in my mind, something is wrong with this picture.

I don't think these children realize their parents won't be around forever so if they don't learn these skills now while their parents are around to help a *Little*, they will be devastated when their parents die. So many of them will go out on their own for a short while, but when times get tough, they're back home. Someone told me of a woman who pays her kids' rent just so they'll stay away. Other parents are buying cars for their kids and pay the insurance as well. I don't blame the kids for not wanting to leave the nest, it's too comfortable. But that's not all there is to life. Besides, I figure after all I've gone through, I deserve the nice place to stay and a new car.

Well in case nobody told them, let me. **Life is tough and sometimes it stays hard for a long time but you have to keep struggling and dealing with it! It will get better!** It was tough

...DNNSMLISE

for all of us but we survived. I think it is my duty to my children to prepare them for the real world. I have already told my kids when they are grown, I will not be at home, they will have to make an appointment to see me and I will only babysit their children when I feel like it. I plan to do all those things I couldn't do when I was trying to raise them. You can ask them. They know I want them to be independent people who can leave my home and only return for visits.

Of course my friends start measuring me for a straight jacket. They don't want me to go off too badly and hurt myself when things don't go the way I planned them. Hey, I know about "The best laid plans of mice and men..." Well I don't care, leave me to my delusions. Hey Jamilah and Askari, eighteen and out! I do believe, I do believe!

Addendum to "Delusions"

Oh alright, I'll admit that Jamilah and Askari may have to move back home, I certainly wouldn't see them living on the streets. Could somebody please check the door and make sure they're not listening in on my conversation. I'm not ready to let them have this information just yet. I conceded to the possibility during a conversation that Gail Harris and I were having. I also stated that during the time they are out of my house ("I do believe, I do believe!"), I was not going to give them a key. Gail politely reminded me it might be for my benefit for them to be able to check on me. Well, if they have to have a key, they have to phone and/or knock on my door before they enter. Hey, think about it, there are all kinds of things I could be doing once they are no longer my responsibility. I could have a man by that time and there was some discussion about swinging from a chandelier. I'd swing just from the joy of having them out of my house! Then I told Gail about my real secret desire on this matter. I would love to have a house big enough that if my children had to move back home, it would have an apartment that they could occupy.

That's when Gail informed me of a new "Level" to work towards. Miss Gail told me the house would not have an apartment, it should be large enough that it would have a separate building called the "Carriage House". Suddenly I had a vision of the original "Sabrina" movie. I remembered Audrey Hepburn and her father (the chauffeur for a rich family), lived over the garage and a very nice place it was indeed. It even had a large tree that Sabrina climbed up to dream of reaching the level of being in the big house. (Didn't you know that there are many of us trying to do that?) Well, now that I have been properly instructed, I am working towards reaching the level that should my children have to move back home, (Hey, somebody check that door again!), they would move into "The Carriage House." It works for me. I do believe, I do believe!

Going Shopping Part 1: The Real Test of Parenting

I realize Askari is no longer a child, he is a young man. I realize that I can no longer just bring clothes home for him to wear without him having some choice in the matter if I expect them to be worn. I even understand that the style is for big clothes. *However,* I am not buying humongous for a boy, oh excuse me, a young man, who is a size 16. Just listen to our latest shopping adventure!

There was a sale on tee shirts at a local department store. I told Askari we were going to get tee shirts and he reminded me

...DNNSMLISE

he needed sneakers. J.T., one of my buddies asked if he could go along for the ride and I said yes. I thought it would be good for Askari to have another male along.

When we got in the store we separated to go look over the merchandise. I told Askari I'd meet him in the boys' department when I finished. I took about twenty minutes to look over some things and then I went looking for Askari. He wasn't in the boys' department. After about ten minutes, I realized I was probably in the wrong section. (I had forgotten who I was dealing with.) I wandered around the store looking for him and found him in the men's department. He had a number of silk boxer shorts in the shopping cart. I reminded him that we were there for tee shirts. He begged and pleaded and I gave in *A Little*. I told him he could get a few and I would have to approve of them. I decided to go do some shoe shopping. I reminded him, he still had to get his sneakers quickly as the three of us were planning to go to a movie in about a hour and a half.

Well you know what they say about the best laid plans of mice and men. They don't work out! By the time I caught up to Askari he had twenty pairs of silk boxers in the shopping cart along with many *Hugh* shirts. I politely let him know that he could only get four pairs of silk boxers. His pediatrician had told me that boxers were better for him than briefs. Askari prefers to sleep in them rather than pajamas so I don't mind. (No, I'm not ready to deal with the fact that they were silk!) Finally I took a look at the size of the articles in the cart and very calmly, I let him know they were all too big. I marched him back to the section of the store he had been in. That's when I realized Askari wasn't in the young men's section, he wasn't in the men's section, he had chosen his clothes from the Tall and Big men's section! That was bad enough. What was worse was that he refused to believe the clothes wouldn't fit him. He swore the shirt he had on, which fit his body, had been purchased from

Don't Need No Soaps, My Life Is Soap Enough!

that section. Nothing that J.T. and I said or did convinced Askari that the clothes were too big. Thanks to Mr. Self Righteous Indignation, we missed the movie.

I remember well the perils of shopping with my mother. She never seemed to understand fashion. In those days, hand-me-downs were a natural part of growing up. In fact, since I was the youngest of nine, the clothes that were passed on to me were so old they had come back in fashion. The other fact of those days was you didn't argue with your mother about how she spent her money on you. Not unless you were on a kamikaze mission! Call me old fashion but I still believe that this should be true. Ask Askari. I refused to buy *Hugh*, but I did agree to buy large. After all, didn't we always promise ourselves we wouldn't do to our kids what our parents did to us. Unless of course, it makes sense!

Just Slit My Wrists and Pass the Pills

Well, I've reached that goal post that many parents have, but I'm not going willingly. Jamilah is now an official college student, and I'm an official poor person. I have no idea how I will pay for her tuition let alone books for the next four years but God willing, I'll find a way. Jamilah is a very talented musician and it has been her saving grace. When I was having all those aforementioned problems, I tried everything to get her back on track. The one thing I didn't take away from her as punishment was her music and I'm glad I didn't. I think she found herself when she began to get involved in music lessons and the band. I publicly want to thank Mr. Kauriga, her music teacher at Girls' High School. I know how important a music teacher can be in a young person's life as I had one in mine. Somehow they seem to be able to understand

...DNNSMLISE

a child when the parent can't. They seem to make the child understand a parent when we can't.

I am also fortunate that Jamilah knows what she wants to major in at college. I've heard of the stories of parents paying large college bills for students who have no idea what they want to be or do. Jamilah not only knows what she wants, she researched and choose her college carefully. In fact, when I would ask her about why she didn't apply to one college or another, she was always able to give me very rational answers about why or how they didn't meet her needs. I had been told at one of the recruitment sessions, that parents need to be careful not to force their child into a college just because they want it. The recruiter pointed out that the student is the one to be on that campus for four years and deal with the professors, curriculum, etc. so the student needs to be happy with the choice.

I could understand that as my parents didn't interfere with my choice of colleges when I was going. It may have been that after nine children they were too tired to say anything. They just kinda' gave me a strange look that I now understand. It's that look that says, "Just slit my wrists and pass the pills. By the time I finish paying for these bills, I'll be too broke to care!" How do I know this? Because I'm beginning to see that look on my face every morning. And I'm just a beginner at this rate.

I went in to see my manager, Louis Malfara, looking for sympathy. I held out my wrists and said "Just start cutting now, I'm signing my life away for a loan for Jamilah. He looked at me without sympathy and glumly said, "Wait until they start messing up on your papers as well!" What could I say, my manager has seven kids, he knows the trials and tribulations well. In fact, I often go to him for wisdom about raising kids. He doesn't have it down to a science but I figured I could learn from his mistakes. Heck, somebody should learn from them and if I can avoid the pain, why not?

DNNSMLISE...

Don't Need No Soaps, My Life Is Soap Enough!

The one thing I keep reminding Jamilah of is that this is no picnic. She added up the cost of getting her degree from the college of her choice and told me the figure. That's when I decided to keep all sharp instruments away from me for the next four years. I calmly told her that anytime she thinks about going to a party when she has work due or cutting a class, she was to divide up what it was costing me to send her there and decide if it was worth the price.

I was talking to my friend, Juanita Stamps, who has a son in college now and another son Askari's age. She said she was more than willing to go live on campus for the four years as the campus was beautiful. To me, that's the key. These young folks have to understand we aren't rich and we are giving up many trips to the islands to help them get a good education. I'm already reminding Jamilah that she *Must* buckle down the first semester. Most students don't make it because of that first semester. If students would hit the books *Hard* that first semester, the rest are easy. But unfortunately, for many students it's pure freedom and not everyone can handle it. It's no more parents, no more books, no more teachers' dirty looks. Heck, why should the teachers care, they get paid no matter what. Books are just something the parents pay for and we never get to see at forty to fifty dollars a shot. It's our dirty looks our children have to be careful of.

Well all I can say is Jamilah better be prepared to hear lecture after lecture from me about the importance of a good college education. I think that's a small price to pay for all the money I have to put out. Does she understand I could probably be a permanent fixture on a beach somewhere if I didn't have these bills? Oh no, I just remembered, Askari is only a few more years behind her!! Hey, why is this knife so dull?!! Quick, pass the gun! Forget about the pills, they're too slow. Oh alright, I'll be realistic. Pass the cookies and don't scrimp on the ice cream.

...DNNSMLISE

53

Askari's Going to MIT

Jamilah, Askari and I were driving somewhere when Askari announced that he was going to go to the University of Pennsylvania (U. of P.) I almost hit a pole because I was trying to reach back to choke him and drive at the same time. It wasn't because I was trying to figure out how I was going to pay for an Ivy League education. That was the last thing on my mind. Remember I have already been introduced to the wonderful world of paying college tuition by Jamilah. I know all my paychecks will belong to some college and only the pay stub will belong to me. No, I was trying to choke him because we live in Philadelphia which is where the U. of P. is located. It would probably be impossible for me to afford the U. of P.'s tuition let alone room and board. That means he wouldn't have to leave home to go to college. That is not in my game plan!

I know I was probably foaming at the mouth as I yelled, "No way, you have to get out of my house! Besides, you are going to MIT (Massachusetts Institute of Technology)", I yelled. Well that set Jamilah off. She started falling out, laughing at the two of us. "Mom," she said, "The kid isn't even in high school yet and you're trying to ship him out!" "Hey, he said he wanted to be a scientist and go to MIT!" I yelled back. Suddenly, Jamilah started straightening up. "Hey wait! He can't go there! I'll be in Massachusetts and I don't want him there." Now I ask you, if they can't stand living together in the same state, how do you think I'm supposed to live with them in the same apartment?!

Meanwhile, Askari hasn't said another word. I guess he figured once again he was caught up between two females and no matter what he said, it would be difficult if not impossible to win. Now this is unusual for Askari. He usually prefers to start mess and confusion and enjoy the ride it causes. He enjoys a challenge! Quietly he suggested that we decide later, he just wanted to get home. What he didn't say was "Meanwhile could you please take your hand off my throat, drive the car and give me a few years to decide." I continued to drive muttering to myself over and over, "Please God, let them go away to college!" This only served to increase my determination that Askari maintain the good grades he is capable of getting so he can receive many scholarship offers. Hey, who said I can't help him plan his life?! Especially if his plans don't include going away from home. I do believe, I do believe! Only time will tell at this point!

More Than I Can Bear

The time has come for me to speak out about the Lord giving me more than I can bear. I know this is not recommended, but this is something I just have to get off my chest. It's not anything major, it was a series of little things that did me in. It started when I made reservations for Jamilah to come home from college. It was with one of those small airlines that are so much more reasonable than the major ones. I had given Jamilah all of her flight information but she called me one day about a week before her scheduled departure. She asked me the name of the airline as she had been to the airport to see a friend off and did not see the name of the airline that I had given her. I called the agent the next day for her to verify the information. That's when we discovered the airline had gone out of business and had not informed us. Of course this was a flight for Christmas, one of the heaviest travel times of the year. The agent was able to get me another reservation but it meant I was paying for a second ticket. A word of caution about paying for airline tickets. If you can, use a credit card, that way if you should run into one of these DNNSMLISE situations you have some protection. You can contact the credit card company which gives you a little more back-up than if you were trying to get a cash refund. But I digress.

I was able to get off from work a little early and I ran to the travel agency to get the tickets. Unlike the cheap airline that operated as a ticketless airline, these tickets had to be sent to Jamilah IMMEDIATELY! The travel agency was charging almost twice what the overnight mail service was going to charge so I had to go running to their office. I won't even talk about the fact that the overnight mail service's office was in Center City Philadelphia and how that location is not conducive to parking. I got a space and managed to get to their office before they closed. I called Jamilah from there to verify some information and that's when she told me that her dorm was officially closed for the holidays and packages were not being accepted. The mailing service did have an office within walking distance of her dorm so I made arrangements for them to hold the package there. They had to deliver the package by the next day, (Christmas Eve) a Tuesday, as that office was closing early and would be closed until the following Monday. Jamilah's flight was going to be on Saturday. Now quickly count with me, that means if delivery wasn't made by the next day, her ticket would be delivered two days late. After verifying the location of the office, time that the package would arrive, and almost threatening Jamilah with death if she didn't get to that office on time the next day, I breathed a sigh of relief as I left their location, confident that Jamilah's trip home was now settled. Yeah right, the story was just beginning.

As soon as I got in the door at home, Askari informed me that the mailing service had called me. Unfortunately, the number he took down wasn't right so I had to call the 800 number.

DNNSMLISE...

Don't Need No Soaps, My Life Is Soap Enough!

Jamilah's Senior Prom Night

...DNNSMLISE

I tried to explain to the service representative that I had just left their downtown office and needed their number. She was not allowed to give me that number and tried to help me by using the package number. It was not registered in the system. After numerous attempts to explain the situation to her, she finally connected me to the downtown office. Remember that the clock is ticking and the office is due to close at anytime. If they close and the package was not shipped, the receiving office would be closed and Jamilah would get her ticket two days late and you know airlines don't honor late tickets but you should be able to get a refund. Are you still following this? Okay I finally get the office on the phone and guess what they wanted? They wanted to know if the directions they had to hold the package at the receiving office were correct? Anybody got a blood pressure cuff handy? No, I did not rant and rave and give them my life history up to this point. I just told them the instructions were correct. I figured the quicker I got them off the phone the quicker Jamilah could get her package.

This is the point where I have to tell you the story gets better. The morning of Jamilah's flight, I had some errands to run. I got an early start and left Askari home. I went to a computer show to purchase some software packages I needed. I called Askari at one point because I needed him to connect me to Gail via the three way phone connections to ask her some questions.

After I had made my purchases, I decided to go past Gail's on my way home to verify the purchases were what I needed. Just as I was ready to leave, Gail's husband told her she had an emergency call. I told Gail to go ahead and get her call and I would talk to her later. I was almost pulling away in my car when Gail came flying out of her house. The emergency call was for me — Jamilah and Askari were on the line. Jamilah was at the airport ready to board the plane for her trip home when the airline informed her she didn't have acceptable identification. She had

Don't Need No Soaps, My Life Is Soap Enough!

her college photo id but they refused to accept it. They would accept her birth certificate which of course is home if I could fax it in time. This was 1:15 P.M. Jamilah's flight was at 1:40 P.M. and I was at least fifteen minutes from home. Gail has a fax machine and quickly volunteered to fax it for me. All I had to do was go home, get and return in, oh say twenty minutes. This is when I earned one of those "Super Mom Badges".

Back to the story. I hopped in my car praying on the way, trying not to drive like a crazy woman. I got to an intersection and the cars are stopped. I'm about the fourth car back and I'm trying desperately to remain calm. I noticed the cars are not moving but the traffic lights are changing. Just as I got ready to start a symphony for one car horn, I noticed that the hold up is being caused by a long funeral. Now, as I said before, God don't like ugly and I think honking at a funeral (no matter what the reason) would be considered ugly. I sat and sat and tried to be glad that the person had so many friends but need I tell you my heart wasn't in it.

Finally I got home and flew into my bedroom to get the needed birth certificate. Askari told me Jamilah had called and was getting a little desperate (she thinks she knows what desperation is? HA!) and suggested I fax the birth certificate from the copying center that was only a few blocks from our apartment. I checked to see if I had money on me to use for the fax (remember I had gone shopping earlier that morning), grabbed the birth certificate and flew up the street in the car. That's when a voice in my head said "Check the birth certificate!" I stopped and looked, I had grabbed Askari's birth certificate. I did an immediate U-turn (yes, I checked for traffic first!) flew back down the street, up the stairs, into my bedroom. I grabbed the right birth certificate, ran back down the stairs, drove up the street, into the copying center's parking lot and now I can't find a close parking space. I grabbed the closest parking space that I

...DNNSMLISE

could, flew up the stairs and into the copying center and yes, you probably guessed it, there was a line of people. Oh yes, I forgot to give you a time check, the time is now 1:35 P.M.

I loudly announced, "Please, can I get in front of everyone because if I don't fax this birth certificate within the next five minutes, my daughter won't be able to come home for the holidays!" I want to thank all of those kinds folks who said "Go ahead!" I managed to get one of the clerks to come over and take my fax as I stood there on pins and needles, praying that I made it on time. When the clerk handed me the fax receipt, I was afraid to look at the time it was received, it said 1:40 P.M. I was relieved and went home to wait a few minutes until I had to leave to pick Jamilah up. When I got home, I thanked Askari for using his head during all of this and especially because he had the foresight to try to locate me at Gail's. When I finished, he informed me that the fax didn't get there in time, Jamilah was trying to contact me and he had informed Gail of the latest events. Of course the pay phone number that Jamilah called from would not take incoming calls. A few minutes later she called to inform me that the airline would not hold up the flight but was putting her on the next flight. Well I did say a quick prayer that she was okay and was only being delayed for a couple of hours. I decided I better get something to eat before I passed out.

Finally, it was time to go get Jamilah. Like most airports, picking up passengers can be an adventure in itself. Need I tell you I was in no mood for another adventure. I had told Jamilah to meet me out front of the arrival terminal for her airline. I got there and waited and waited and waited. Well you can guess that I was panicking that she had missed her flight. I kept checking the board announcing the arrival times of the flights. By the time I realized that at least one other flight from her city had arrived, the panic was in full bloom. I asked one of the police officers that was directing traffic how I could page a passenger.

Don't Need No Soaps, My Life Is Soap Enough!

He took me over to the appropriate phone and I quickly paged her, praying all the time that I wasn't given a ticket for abandoning my car. When Jamilah came out of the terminal, I was so frazzled that I could barely give her a good welcome home hug. Besides, I was too busy formulating the letter I was going to send to the Lord about how I didn't think I was being unreasonable to consider this whole chain of events as being too much too bear. But, I'm a punk and the last person a punk like me wants to have mad at her is the Lord! That's why you had to suffer through this chapter. Hey, until you can show me that you pack lightening bolts and pestilence, I figured having you listen to my tale of woe is a whole lot safer!

Becoming a Trend Setter

Believe me it was never my intention to be a trend setter. It was another of those realities of life that snuck up on me. The trend setting I'm talking about is wearing my kids hand-me-downs. Now I already told you I was the youngest in a family of nine children so naturally, I was use to hand-me-downs. Remember I also mentioned that the hand-me-downs were so old they had come back in fashion so I really didn't mind. Hey, I could be one of the hip crowd (there I go again telling my age by the words I use!) but you understand what I mean. However, I thought when I became a grown-up, had a job and became a parent, those days of hand-me-downs were a distant memory. HA! How many times do I have to remind myself, "Who said life is fair?"

The trend setting is only coming about because I am a small person and my children are larger than me. Like most parents, I had continued that family tradition of hand-me-downs when I

...DNNSMLISE

passed on a few of Jamilah's unisex items to Askari while they were babies. I am not a sewer but I managed to make a few pairs of pants for Jamilah when she was a baby. Jamilah was such a tiny baby that it didn't take much material to make them. They were very simple, a few seams and an elastic band at the top. You know the kind you really can't tell if they are for a boy or a girl — unisex. They were quite roomy for her even with her diaper on. I saved them and thought I'd be able to show my handiwork off again when Askari was born. Hey, come on now. How much difference is there between girls and boy pants that have snaps on the inside leg of them? I quickly realized there was going to be a major difference between my two children that had nothing to do with their sex. It had every thing to do with their size. The poor boy couldn't even bend down in the pants. That was a clear indication that he would be larger than she was. Okay, I knew that from the time they were born since he was larger even then. Remember delusions have helped me survive, why should I get rid of them now?

But the trend of me wearing **their** hand-me-downs was years away yet. The first stage of hand-me-downs was between Jamilah and Askari But by the time they well into their adolescence, it was clear that Askari would soon be the biggest member of the household. I remember when Jamilah began to inherit Askari's sneakers and boots because his feet were just slightly larger than hers. Now he has no competition for his cast off footwear. But his clothes are another story. There was a time that Jamilah could give him her old jeans, now it's the other way around. There was a fierce battle one summer when Askari went to throw away some of his old clothes and Jamilah found the bag before it went out. She was merrily planning new outfits with some of his old shirts when Askari realized what was going on. Mind you, he could no longer wear these things but he was not ready to see his sister walking around in them. Me, I want my money's

Don't Need No Soaps, My Life Is Soap Enough!

worth from any article I buy so I saw no problem. But Brother Man did. I finally put my foot down, small as it may be, and decided that Jamilah could keep them when even Askari had to admit they fit her.

My trend setting began when I bought Askari a very nice down-filled coat one winter. Up until that time, I had been able to get two years worth of wear from their clothes. I knew it wouldn't last forever but after a couple of years of this, I was good and spoiled. So it was an unexpected surprise when Askari announced that his winter coat from last year didn't fit. At first I thought he was just trying a fashion ploy to get a new coat because I knew he didn't like the coat anymore. But he was right, the coat did fit him a little snug. Alright, I decided, you have to admit Askari is no longer going to get two years wear from every piece of clothing I bought.

I was prepared to pass the coat on until I realized it would fit me. Not only would it fit, I could accessorize it very nicely. But it was a hand-me-down! Hadn't I past that stage of life? Am I not a grown-up? Don't I work every day so I can pay for things including clothes for me? Don't I get to pick my own clothes? Don't I deserve a new coat? Don't I need to get a grip? After once again admitting that the rule of life not being fair applies to me as well, I had to do a reality check. Hey, this was not the end of the world, just a temporary setback! Besides I had to admit, the coat fit nicely and was quite warm. I had to realize that I won't always get new clothes if hand-me-downs are available. But you know I had figured out a way to maintain my pride and self respect! So I have begun practicing the following speech: "Askari, from now on I have to approve your choice of clothes and you will have to take better care of them because one day, they may be mine!!!"

...DNNSMLISE

My Revenge

I have often heard parents tell their children they hope they have children just like they (the children) were. I now understand why they say that. One of my girlfriends proudly displays a poster that says "Get revenge on your children, live long enough to be a problem to them." I don't want to do that, I want to live long enough not to be involved in their problems. My plan is to be too busy traveling to cause them a problem.

My children and I went to see "A League Of Their Own". The opening scene shows the daughter trying to get her mother to go to the reunion of the female baseball players. The mother has cocooned herself in her room after the death of her husband. I turned to my kids and said "You won't have to worry about me being stuck in a room." They said "You're right, we'd kick you out." See, that's why we get along so well, they understand me!

One day my kids got on my last good nerve so I told them that one day they would have children of their own. The day would come when their children were giving them a hard way to go and they were going to call me and want to know what they should do. "And you know what I will tell you?" I asked. They said "What?" I said "HA! HA! HA! and you have to pay me for the advise." They said "That's cold!" And I said "Yes it is, but that's how I get my revenge." Besides, that's one way to pay for my trips.

I told Jamilah one day (after a particularly trying time) that I understand she can't really appreciate all that I do for her now. However, I have instructed her and her brother that when they turn twenty-five they are each to throw me a big party in appre-

Don't Need No Soaps, My Life Is Soap Enough!

ciation of all I had to put up with. They are to invite all of my friends because if it wasn't for them letting me know "This too shall pass" or at least giving me a murmur of understanding, we may not have survived. And in the event that I don't make it to that day, they have been instructed to throw the party for my friends. Those of you who have helped me keep my sanity while raising my children, stay in touch, we've got a party to go to!

...DNNSMLISE

DNNSMLISE...   Bea Joyner

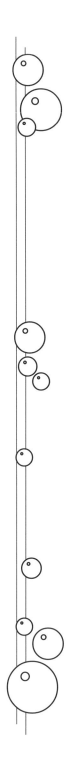

DNNSMLISE...

PART THREE:
SURVIVAL TECHNIQUES

"Generations" Alphonsa Joyner

...DNNSMLISE

DNNSMLISE...   Bea Joyner

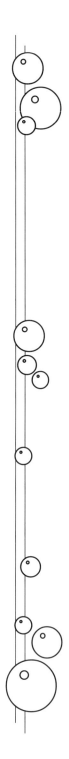

DNNSMLISE...

Survival Technique #1
Going to the Movies On My Lunch Break

I am an avid movie buff. I love going to the theater and watching all kinds of films (horror excluded.) When my children were younger, I had a hard time getting to see the movies I wanted. I discovered that I could go to the movies on my lunch hour. I simply used the lunch hour plus two or three hours of my vacation time depending on the length of the film and the location of the theater. It was Great! I got to see the movies I wanted at a matinee price, without being worried about being out at night by myself. There were no baby-sitter fees and my manager got one happy worker. Plus, I only had two or three more hours of work when I got back. Fortunately, my manager understood because he has a large family. As long as it didn't interfere with my work schedule, he had no problems. He just shook his head the first time I told him what I was doing. In fact, it got to the point where I would tell him I was overdue to go to the movies!

I'd pack my lunch up, buy a soda there and for two to three hours, I could lose myself in another world. I saw some great comedies which did a lot to keep my sanity intact. Once, on my way back, a man commented on how much I was grinning as he had come from the same movie. It was a great movie and for a short time I could forget my troubles and not worry about anything, except getting back on time. Imagine going to see Bette Midler and Danny DiVito in "Outrageous Fortunes" or "The Empire Strikes Back" on your lunch break. I did!

You do need to be careful what movie you go see. I went to see "Die Hard 2". A friend was going to try to go with me but

...DNNSMLISE

he wasn't able to get away. As soon as I got back, I called him. I began to realize something was wrong because he just kept saying "Uh huh, that's nice." Suddenly it dawned on me I was all hyped up from the movie. It was a great action movie and I was so excited I didn't even realize how "hyped" I was. But boy was I easy to get along with that day!

Survival Technique #2
Cheap Therapy... Reading Cards in the Card Shops

On those days when I need a break and I can't get away for a movie, I head for the nearest card shop. I just head for the funny card section and read away. I have bought more cards that way, saving them for the right person. I have a couple of friends with whom I have birthday card battles. Sometimes, I find a card a year in advance for just the right person. One year the card shop in my building had such great cards, I made my girl friend come over and pick out her favorite. There were just too many to choose from. She thought I was crazy until she got in the shop and started howling. I had to leave before she embarrassed me and I wouldn't be able to return. After all, I didn't want them thinking I was crazy.

Card reading is great fun and like any other window shopping, you don't have to buy. I was nearly in hysterics one day at a large department store, when a woman started talking to me. By that time, I had tears rolling down my face from laughing. She told me I had a wonderful smile. I thanked her and kept right on reading and laughing. Try it sometimes!

My Only Vices are Cookies and Ice Cream

My friends think I'm crazy when I tell them my only vices are cookies and ice cream or as I call them "C&C". Drugs are a definite no-no, and I don't think it is very practical to try to smoke when I'm choking to death. I can't drink, it doesn't agree with my body. I found that out the hard way. It only took a couple of trips to "Europe" for me to make a pact with my body. (The trip to "Europe" is when you find yourself hugging the toilet as you throw-up everything in your body. The only sound you're capable of making is the word "Europe!") I won't put liquor in my body and my body has agreed it won't make me cry out for death. I simply stick to cookies and ice cream!

I love to make homemade cookies. In fact, my girlfriend's grandmother has nicknamed me "Cookie Bea". Now you know, if Grandma says I'm good, I'm good. I make all kinds - sugar, peanut butter and of course chocolate chip. Sometimes, I give them out as Christmas gifts. One man told me my cookies were better than sex, I doubt that but they are good. On rare occasions (usually in the summer when it's too hot to turn on the oven), I am forced to buy cookies. Don't get me wrong, there are some good store cookies, I just happen to be a cookie connoisseur. I'm particular about the cookies I eat. For example, Pathmark Super Market sells a good old fashion vanilla sandwich cookie. Pepperidge Farms has a good brownie cookie and their Chessman cookies are hard to beat. However, they can keep their large cookies, it just doesn't do it for me. And Mrs. Fields Cookies! The kids and I were on our way to Baltimore with a friend and her son when I spied a sign for Mrs. Fields cookies at the rest stop. I announced that we would stop on the

...DNNSMLISE

way back and I would buy **Me** some cookies. True to my word, I did. I satisfied my kids by giving them money for the video games. But I had my cookies!

A few years ago, a friend introduced me to Seventh Heaven ice cream. It's only made and sold in Trenton, New Jersey. In my opinion, it's better than Ben & Jerry's and Breyers and it's a lot cheaper. They make more flavors than I ever heard of. They have whole sections just for all the varieties of strawberry, chocolate, and nut flavors. Have you ever tried Cashew and Caramel that melts in your mouth for only 99 cents a pint? How about Strawberry Amaretto? Chocolate with M&M's? Raspberry Turbulence? Chocolate Butter Pecan? Only 99 cents!

Every so often, I make an ice cream run. It generally takes about two hours to go and come back. My children will put in their order. They're allowed to get one pint for themselves but of course as soon as it's gone, they're in the half gallon. Usually I'll get three or four half gallons as I can store them in my ice cream buddies' deep freezer. I think it might be dangerous for me to get my own freezer! I'll call them up when I'm all out and say "It's time for an ice cream run!" Everyone calls me crazy until they taste it. I have yet to find one person who doesn't like it.

Think of it this way, cookies and ice cream are cheaper than a diamond ring and as long as you don't go over board, you can eat it. That's the trick, you can't go hog wild, it's too rich for that. Moderation is the key. I may talk a good game, but I know where cookies and ice cream go in their after life, right on my hips and thighs! So I take it easy, maybe one or two scoops a night. That's the limit. Hey, how far would you go for a nice cold beer or that cigarette. I rest my case!

DNNSMLISE...

Exercising with Joanie Greggins

I've been a person in constant motion all of my life. I was born at home because my mother couldn't get to the hospital quick enough. Even my childhood nickname had to do with speed, "Roadrunner". I rarely walked when I could run when I was a kid. I love track, basketball, anything with speed within reason. I'd love to get up the nerve to try to toboggan but I'm not about to jump off a mountain like the skiers do.

One of my girl friends, Dorothy Coles was heavy. She went on vacation to the islands and had a bicycle accident. She broke her leg and the examining doctor told her in a very disgusted voice, "You have to lose weight!" She got so angry that she decided to do just that. We were about the same height so she made my weight her goal. She changed her diet and began to exercise regularly. Now you know how people are once they get on the "bandwagon". Well once she got down to and below my weight she began making surprise inspections of my desk drawer at work. At that time I would keep three to four different kinds of cookies in my desk. Now instead of coming to get some, she came to lecture me. It's hard to argue with someone who had been heavy and was now looking better than me. She kept telling me to watch Joanie Greggins. I've always enjoyed exercising so I decided to give it a try.

Joanie Greggins is the female Jack LaLanne. (For those too young to know or too embarrassed to admit knowing who he is, Jack was the exercising guru for many decades.) Here was this woman who could do a vigorous work-out while talking a mile a minute and never run out of air! I was fascinated. I became a faithful watcher. At that time she was coming on at 6:30 A.M. Then she moved to 6:00 A.M. The last time I saw her, the show was on at 5:30 A.M. and I was hanging tough. I enjoyed her because she would always tell you to do what you could and don't try to kill yourself. She would give you an alternative way of doing the exercise but she was like a drill sergeant. She reminded me of some of my former gym teachers.

Joanie Greggins was living proof of what she stressed. Her body was gorgeous and I was jealous. I wanted my body to look just like hers. However I finally came to my senses and realized my body would never look like hers because I wasn't willing to exercise eight hours a day or more the way she did. Besides I found out she was a former gym teacher, and that explained it for me. **However,** Joanie had a saying that has stuck with me. She would have us on the floor doing leg and thigh lifts and she'd say "You grew it, you lift it." It's hard to argue with that kind of logic. I looked down and I could see cheese steaks and pizzas just under the skin lurking there like the creature from "Predator" and the worst part was I knew I had let him in.

Well I have cut back tremendously on cheese steaks and we only do pizzas once in a while. I regularly eat salads and watch what I eat but I refuse to give up my cookies and ice cream. That was the only consolation I had when Joanie was whipping me into shape. I knew that later that evening I would be rewarding myself with dessert but of course knowing I had to lift what I grew, I did so in moderation. And Dorothy, well I'm proud to say, went on to become an instructor for Weight Watchers and wears a diamond pin — her reward for losing so much weight. But she still can't convince me to give up cookies and ice cream even when she pulls out the measuring tape!

"Getting to the Level" or...
My First Buying Trip to Victoria's Secret

Getting to the Level is a very important concept that my friend Nina Bryant taught me. Actually Toni Cade Bambara was the first one to put me on the right road when she was my professor in college. She explained to us that color T.V., air conditioning and wall to wall carpeting were not luxuries, they were necessities. Nina's explanation was that you will know you are at the "Level" when you can afford to have someone else clean your house **Regularly**, bills are not a problem, and luxury items are common place, but especially when you have underwear that matches all the time.

I had been trying to get to the "Level" for a long time but I knew I wasn't there because I had a difficult time just keeping enough Hanes underwear in the house for all of us. Of course I had heard of Victoria's Secret, I just wasn't near enough to the "Level" to even go window shopping there. I have a problem about doing things that will cause me to hurt myself. If I can't afford to pay the price of things, I don't go drooling over them and therefore cause myself to get totally disgusted with the way my life is going. It's not a good idea to keep calling the Lord up and complaining. (See my introduction).

Some of my girlfriends had been singing the praises of Victoria's Secret, how wonderful the underwear was, how feminine it made them feel. Of course they weren't in my "shoes" as their children were grown and almost gone or married, meaning they had the money to spend. No, I won't list my bills to prove my point. All I kept saying was "Someday". My friend Gail was more persistent because she knows I deserve better. She understands me. She is also the one who reminds me to be

...DNNSMLISE

flexible and try different things. She designed some of my poems as individual pieces which sold in a local art gallery so of course I have to listen to her. Gail took me shopping with her one day after work as she had some items to return to Victoria's Secret. I was free to browse while she made her purchases. I was ready to leave when I heard someone say something about "$28" panties. I started trying to remember if Hanes underwear was on sale that week.

I can't deny how beautiful the items were at Victoria's Secret but they aren't cheap. However, "Victoria", being the sales mogul that she is, has two for two sales on most of her undies. I saw beautiful lounging outfits, robes, and nightgowns that were ready to be taken on any honeymoon. I tried to at least act like I was at the "Level" but when the saleswoman said something about "The Bra Room", I had to start cutting up. By then Gail was in "The Bra Room" looking at the "Wonder Bra" which is designed to give cleavage to those of us who thought that was only in our dreams. I did have to say very quietly to Gail, "Where were they when we needed them?" It's very obvious that most young ladies today have had cleavage since they were in elementary school!

I promised Gail I would go back and actually buy something from Victoria's Secret and she agreed to go with me. I knew it was time when "Brother Man" Askari decided to get heavy into his "unappreciation" stage and "Girl Friend" Jamilah was complaining about how bad his attitude was. I have to admit, nothing inspires me to go spend some money on myself as much as that combination does.

It was a good thing Gail did go with me because it quickly became apparent that I was not on the "Victoria Level". I was trying to be good, honest I was! I even told Gail "No cotton drawers, right?" We headed for the very nice, very silky, two-for-two panties table. I knew I had seen at least three or four

Don't Need No Soaps, My Life Is Soap Enough!

different kinds. I was not prepared for the ten or more kinds. I agreed to get at least four panties and a couple of two for two bras. I thought I'd get the printed panties as I didn't have any of those. I was trying to be flexible! I quickly got my four panties, stopped by "The Bra Room" for a few bras and headed for the dressing room. There was no way I was going to get any of these things without trying them on.

Fortunately for me, the dressing rooms are locked and individual or Gail might have disowned me. I tried the panties on first. I knew that was a mistake. It's hard to get the right effect when you put them on over Hanes. It's just not the same. I knew as soon as I saw them on, there was not enough material in the right places. There are some things that a woman knows about her body without anyone telling her and that's one I know. I made myself a promise that the Ski Machine I was buying would get a good work out this winter. You don't have to make any snide remarks. You're talking to a woman who enjoys getting up at 5:00 A.M. to exercise. I was more excited about getting that machine than I was about anything I saw in Victoria's. I even saw a nice workout outfit I was thinking about getting.

Well, I was fine until Gail started passing me bras over the door. I never thought my breasts were lopsided until I starting trying on Miss Victoria. Actually, I thought Queen Victoria had designed some of them, they were so hard to get into them. I finally figured out that the straps were set at the tightest fitting. That helped some but not enough. I'm not willing to wear anything that feels like a torture chamber, I don't care how pretty it is.

Gail also passed me some of those ten different kinds of panties. I didn't want to tell her, but I couldn't figure some of them out. I heard a couple of D.J.'s describe women's swimwear as "Butt Floss". Made perfect sense to me! However, the only thing I floss is my teeth. I kept trying to be flexible and I was more comfortable with them when I realized it's the lace side

...DNNSMLISE

up. No wonder men have such a hard time trying to buy these things for us by themselves! I quickly rejected any that didn't have enough material, but finally Gail passed me a couple of pairs that passed my standards.

But those damn bras were another matter! I was really beginning to wonder if I should see a plastic surgeon about the lopsided problem. Gail finally got around to passing me a "Wonder Bra" It's a wonder alright. I hate padded bras. I don't care if I'm small, it's me or nothing. But I remembered about being flexible. I was flexible alright. I quickly thanked the designers when I realized I could take the padding out. And you know what, they fit me better.

There was still a problem with the lopsidedness. I realized I was in trouble, so I had to ask Gail to take a look. She quickly showed me the trick to the lopsidedness - you bend over! I couldn't believe it, the bra fit like it should. I know we have a tendency to curse gravity but sometimes there is a valid reason for it. I finally found a couple of bras that fit (bend over fool!) and I was willing to try. We found panties I could wear and matched them to the two bras I was getting. I promised myself that I would be back, but most of the good stuff is going to have to wait until the Ski Machine has moved in and we're on real good terms!

Going to the Professionals for Make-Up

You have to understand, that trip to Victoria's Secrets was not the first time that a friend had tried to turn me on to the world of female beauty secrets. In fact, I was deeply involved in it myself when I was in junior high school. I faithfully got up every morning to apply makeup. I had a regime of

Don't Need No Soaps, My Life Is Soap Enough!

green eye shadow, eyeliner (the kind you had to put on with a paint brush), mascara, and lipstick. I even used the face creams just like in the commercials. And I knew I looked good!

Unfortunately, it didn't last too long. I got tired of the hours it required to apply that gook and I resented people asking me where was my face if I didn't have any makeup on. I decided my face was on at all times and I wasn't going to cover it up any more. (Yes, Jamilah, I was about thirteen years old wearing makeup. Just remember I am your mother, you aren't mine. Besides you didn't have to deal with my mother!) I think the final deciding factor was how old it was making me look. I know, at that age most young girls want to look older. I looked older in my junior high school pictures than I did in my high school graduation picture!

Over the years other females have tried to convince me how much better I would look if I would just apply a little makeup. Their idea of a little and mine were very far apart. Their idea of a little usually consisted of eye shadow, eye liner, mascara, foundation, blush, and lipstick. My idea of a little was none. I usually won out. I have to admit my looks do improve with makeup especially with eye make-up. That's not the problem. The basic problem is I'm lazy. I don't want to take the time to do it. I still have flashbacks of my junior high school days. It doesn't matter to me that the makeup industry has greatly improved, I haven't.

Every once in a while, (usually decades) I decide to try makeup again. In those rare instances, I'll go and get the few things I'm not too lazy to use. I'll even go for the good stuff. Once I even bought a huge make-up kit. They're all stored somewhere in the back of my closet. I can tell they've been there awhile because the mascara is usually all dried out before I remember where it is. It doesn't matter to me that I've paid a lot of money for something that sees more of my closet than my face. Hey, when I'm tired of it, that's it.

...DNNSMLISE

DNNSMLISE... *Bea Joyner*

One girlfriend thought she had the answer to keep me in makeup. She felt if I was professionally made up, I would see the light and finally join the millions of other women in spending hours in front of the mirror faithfully. I agreed to go to the cosmetic counter to let the experts try their skills. I decided to take a male friend with me since most of us do this to attract males. I thought it would be helpful to get a second opinion. So off we went to department store on our lunch hour.

As you might have guessed, I was not on my best behavior. My girlfriend knew exactly what I needed and so did the sales clerk. Unfortunately, nobody asked me. I tried my best not to laugh but it's hard not to when you're being painted up. It didn't help that the counter was out in the open (what makeup counter isn't) and everyone going by was giving their opinion of the situation by their facial expressions. I have to give the sales clerk credit, she did her best but she made no sale that day. She finally gave up because I had started laughing so hard, I had tears running down my face. Both of my friends tried hard to get me to act right and be properly made up but it didn't help. I think Askari's comment said it all when I picked him up from the daycare that day. He was about four years old at the time. He looked up and me and said "What's wrong with your face?" Out of the mouths of babes!

Right now, I'm back into makeup a LITTLE bit. I am wearing lipstick. I now have to put on the lipstick liner, lipstick and finish with the lip gloss. I admit, it looks good. Just don't be surprised when you don't see it after awhile. Laziness is sure to return sometime soon!

Don't Need No Soaps, My Life Is Soap Enough!

I'm Waiting on Ed McMahon

I've decided there has to be a better way to live my life than this. Actually I was waiting on "Prince Charming" but a male friend informed me that the white horse stumbled and both he and "Prince Charming" fell and broke their necks. So much for riding off into the sunset.

I have been trying to get on the "Sugar Daddy" mailing list. Hey, I just want the chance to prove that money won't make me happy. I know people have said it doesn't, I just want to prove it to myself. Another male friend told me that won't work because I'd be trying to tell the "Sugar Daddy" what I won't do. He must have had the mailing lists mixed up. I'm looking for the one where some man is willing to spend some money on me with no strings attached. I decided when I got my apartment, if some man wanted to pay my rent, I wouldn't let him. He could pay the gas, electric or any other bill but not the rent. If I got tired of his nonsense before the end of the month and told him he had to leave, I didn't want to hear anything about he paid the rent that month and he wasn't leaving. He was going!

My male friend said that was a perfect example of what he was talking about. He doesn't understand. I'm not looking for a millionaire boyfriend like Donald Trump or the owner of the Redskins. I'm looking for someone who doesn't mind spending a little money on me for the pleasure of my company. Besides, since I'm not at the "Level", I think I'd be a real bargain. Believe me, I've outgrown Smokey Robinson's "Could You Love A Poor Boy". The answer is yes, I have and I'm still paying the cost.

I'm also on the lookout for the "Secret Underground of Reasonable and Sensible Males". I believe in my heart of hearts there is an underground of males who know how to treat a lady

...DNNSMLISE

and are looking for ladies who can appreciate them. I know there are some real good guys out there, I've met them from time to time. They are searching for someone to spend their time (hopefully some money) and even their lives with. Everytime I mention this underground to males (for some reason, it always seems to be married men), they swear there is no such place. I calmly inform them there is but the location was changed and their key was taken away when they got married.

But getting back to Ed McMahon. Since "Prince Charming" died and the "Sugar Daddy" list isn't available, I was open to suggestions. And there it was in my mailbox. Ed was going to come to somebody's house with a very large check and I couldn't think of any reason why it shouldn't be mine. I dutifully filled out all the mailings and sent them in right away. I was cheerfully informed that I have beaten out millions of others, and if I ordered some magazines, I'll be placed in the Winners' Circle. Now at first the only requirement was to mail in the envelope. I figured it was cheaper to put a 29 cents stamp on an envelope than playing the lottery and my chances couldn't get any worst. However, it has progressed to threats of taking me out of the exclusive circle of only a few hundred thousand if I don't order right away.

My poor coffee table is overflowing at this very moment from all the magazines I have ordered. I do have some restraint. I will order a magazine for one year and after that, I'm done. I saw it as an opportunity to expose my children to a variety of publications. We have had Life, Newsweek, U. S. News, and Ebony. I faithfully re-order Essence and American Photo. I figured I'm a permanent fixture in the American Family Publishers mailroom. Ha! Your membership to that exclusive circle is only as permanent as your last order.

Now to be fair, you don't have to buy to participate. But I'd advise you to take a close look at that return form you have to send in if you don't order. The card doesn't even have a return address on it! I get the impression my chance of moving from the Winners' Circle to the one in a million winner will improve greatly if I order something... anything! I try to be rational about my chances of winning even if I do order something. The fine print that details the ratio of your chances for winning is too small for me to read. And I'd be the first to admit that Ed McMahon is not my idea of "Prince Charming". My idea of "Prince Charming" is someone who is over six feet tall, with dark or golden brown skin (or any chocolate hue), gray eyes, a body to die for, etc. etc. It is not some white man over the age of sixty-five who looks like he may not make it to the next drawing. But hey, until I get on that "Sugar Daddy" mailing list, Ed McMahon looks real good about now. Hey Ed, me next!

Jamilah Tries to Burst My Bubble

Jamilah has just tried to burst my bubble. She calmly announced to me that I should give up on Ed McMahon. I can't seem to convince her how wonderful life will be once Ed shows up. Usually this is while I'm busy trying to figure out how to remain in that winning circle without ordering another magazine, video or other trinket he has taken to hocking. Doesn't she understand that Ed is going to help me "get to the Level" in one fell swoop. Otherwise, it's going to take some time.

Getting to the "Level" in the real world doesn't happen overnight. It's usually a series of steps that are sometimes so subtle, you don't even realize it's happened. That's why I've been busy trying to get and keep my life in order. I know that getting to the "Level" happens to those who prepare themselves for it. That's why I've gone back to graduate school to increase my market-

...DNNSMLISE

able skills. That's why I keep on Jamilah and Askari about their grades so they can keep on the right track of preparing themselves to go to a good college. And, of course, so they can get a good job and stay out of my house.

Sometimes though, we've worked so hard to get to the "Level" that when we've finally arrived, we deny we've reached it, as if we don't deserve it. We keep checking around to see if it's really us who made it. We won't spend our hard earned cash on something just to celebrate what we have accomplished. I have friends whose job it is to remind me to celebrate me in meaningful ways. Theodore L. Bryant, whom I call Ted, is still working on me being able to surprise him one day with a call from the islands telling him I've decided to treat me right. Somehow the bills keep getting in the way of that plan. Well, after all I've been through, I know I deserve. That's why I want it in one fell swoop, Ed waltzing into my house with wine and checks.

Jamilah is a stubborn kind of person at times. She is known to have a mean streak in her too. I think that's why she told me very matter-of-factly as only the young can do, "Ed's going to croak before he shows up at our door. Why do you think he's advertising life insurance now. He's going to take out a policy and then he's going to croak. I can see him in his casket now." she stated as she folded her arms and had this look on her face that I had a hard time placing. Then I realized that's how Ed looks now. Somehow her argument was beginning to make sense. No, no, I do believe! I do believe! Doesn't she understand the virtues of positive thinking? Hey, he shows up at all those other houses, why not ours. Oh no! Maybe that's it, he doesn't do apartments! But that can't be, after all his mail comes faithfully to my mail box almost every month announcing the big sweepstakes. Hey, if I can't have my delusions of having my children leaving home, can't Ed at least show up?!!

DNNSMLISE...

Don't Need No Soaps, My Life Is Soap Enough!

Oh, About That Ski Machine...!

Just as I was about to order that ski machine, Daveda called me. "How would you like to work out with a personal trainer?", she asked. I thought either Ed McMahon had shown up or I had reached the "Level" and nobody had bothered to tell me. I had always heard how high the rates were for a personal trainer. Only in my dreams did I imagine that I would ever hear those magic words, "Harder, harder! Okay, now give me twenty more!" Daveda assured me that the rates were reasonable. So what did I have to lose? I called Eric Bonner, the trainer, and after a few pleasantries and questions I told him in no uncertain terms, "Listen, I'll do anything you ask, just leave my cookies and ice cream alone!" Hey, a woman's got to put her foot down sometimes!

For the past few years, I had been living in someone else's body. It had to be the body of someone else, 'cause it sure didn't look like mine. I know those rolls around my waist didn't belong to me, I just couldn't find anyone to return them to. And no one was showing up on my door steps saying, "Excuse me, I think I left ten to fifteen pounds of blubber on your waist. Do you mind giving them back now? I really miss them." Have you ever heard any body claim they woke up and mysteriously found themselves in a gorgeous body. No one wakes up screaming "Help, I'm trapped in Ms. Universe's body." Of course not! Only those blubber bodies seem to take over someone else.

So off to Eric's I went. As I said before, God looks after babies and fools and I haven't been a baby in a long time. And Eric turned out to be a godsend. He explained to me that he not only believes in exercising but a proper diet as well. He gave me a questionnaire to find out what state my health was in. He told me that how I eat is just as important as what I eat. He gave me written instructions and I entered a new phase in my life... drinking gallons of water. I had always resisted that eight glasses of water a day theory. Ever since I was pregnant with Jamilah, my bladder has constantly been working over time. I had visions of floating away on an ocean of water should I ever attempt those giant glasses. Depends commercials (for adult diapers) have me shaking that they may be needed sooner that I want. Eric carefully explained that I might not drink eight glasses but increasing my intake of water would help my system eliminate waste that had gathered in my body from years of improper eating. He assured me that my lower back problems would ease if I allowed my system to flush out the impurities. I had an immediate vision of being this bent over old lady trying to struggle down the street. That was enough to convince me to try his regiment.

I have always loved to exercise so that part wasn't hard for me to accept. My knees and sometimes my shoulders thought they should be free to voice their opinion on the matter. They moaned and groaned and cracked and squeaked but Eric and I were persistent and consistent. Eventually they got the message and slowly I discovered my body again.

I think the first three weeks were the hardest. The more Eric tried to convince me to give up my cookies and ice cream, the more I ignored him. I had gotten a new half gallon of Seventh Heaven and I refused to let go. Finally I told him, "Look, we have to come to some kind of agreement. I'll admit I've been acting like a spoiled brat. I've had more ice cream in the past two weeks than I have in months. And I'm paying for it because that much ice cream is making me lactose intolerant." I had to explain how they were my only vices! Eric asked me to tell him everything I had eaten for the past couple of days so he could see what I was doing. I tried to tell him I suffer from CKT

Don't Need No Soaps, My Life Is Soap Enough!

(Can't Keep Track). He told me to write it down. I could tell he had heard that excuse before.

That's when I discovered I have a terrible sweet tooth. But I try to do it in moderation. I could follow Eric's plan faithfully until the evening hours. I drank my water. I consumed the proper amounts of fruits, vegetables and carbohydrates. However the last item on the list was hot apple pie and ice cream (Hey, I ran out of cookies!) I tried to sneak that part of the list past him but he heard me loud and clear. Fortunately, Eric discovered I wasn't as bad as I was talking. I haven't forgotten about those "Predator Thighs"! He realized I talked a good game but I wasn't going overboard. I did see his eyebrows go up when I got to the part about the pie and ice cream. He began to back off a little when I informed him that I was getting back into clothes I hadn't been able to wear in a while. It was that other person's body that wouldn't fit, I knew mine would. And we both celebrated when I announced I had lost eighteen pounds. That was the day he told me I could celebrate with ice cream, but with moderation of course!

Gail is Making Me Wear Make-up and I Protest!

Have you ever had a friend who won't take no for an answer? Well, that's Gail. I can't seem to convince her that I don't need make-up, even for a special occasion. I don't know what's wrong with that, I happen to like my face naked. It's survived all these many years (don't be impolite, how many is not the issue!) without a daily regiment of make-up but Gail won't take no for an answer.

We were discussing what I was going to wear for a reading. I was quite content to discuss what shoes, suit and sash I was

...DNNSMLISE

going to wear. I should have known something was up when I said I was going to wear my off white suit with a lace body suit and red shoes. I was suspicious when I heard the pause in Gail's voice. I've had years of practice of escaping females who want me to join the ranks of women who spend their whole life at the make-up counter. Well, most of their time is spent there, at least it seems that way to me. Anyway, Gail politely told me that the red shoes would draw too much attention to my feet and not enough to my words. I hadn't thought of it that way, I had a one track mind. I thought the red would be a nice contrast to my outfit. I wasn't worried about the audience watching my feet. I don't think they are that eye catching. Okay, I agreed to wear the off white shoes. I thought I was done. Gail was just beginning.

Next we had to discuss lipstick. I told Gail I would wear the pink stuff I got when we went to the department store. I thought she was going to hyperventilate. She couldn't imagine where I got pink lipstick from. I tried to explain and finally I pulled the case out and read her the color — it was berry or burgundy as Gail told me. Hey, what do you want from me, it wasn't red, therefore it was pink. Suddenly I had visions of all those females who have been after me for years sending Gail more energy to continue the battle. She asked about the rest of my make-up and poor unsuspecting me said, I thought I wouldn't wear any because I have a tendency to laugh a lot and that causes lots of tears (of joy of course). She wasn't having any of it. She started discussing water proof eye make up. She didn't realize she was about to be talking to herself because I was setting up my escape route. "There's nothing wrong with a naked face", I claimed. "Oh yes there is and you might as well get used to wearing make-up because when you start making appearances, and especially on T.V., you have to wear it.", Gail explained.

DNNSMLISE...

Don't Need No Soaps, My Life Is Soap Enough!

It's amazing to me how calm these females can be when trying to convince me that make-up will become a part of my life. I could see the "Stepford Wives" or "The Invasion of the Body Snatchers" coming after me. I feel the same way about make-up that I do about those creatures — run or pretty soon none of the real you will be around for long. I threatened to write her up in this book again. "So what!", she told me as she started discussing water proof eye make-up remover. I know I thought to myself, I have a good answer. "Besides", I said "Whoopi Goldberg doesn't wear make-up!" "Oh yes she does", Gail quickly told me. "She had to get used to it too. Now she pays other people to put it on for her." I could tell I was losing this battle. Maybe this is why I never was real close friends with women who believe make-up will cover up any flaw. I'd rather work on the flaw and forget the cover up. I don't care if it's a permanent flaw that would look better with a little help, covering it up is too much work for me. Gail started talking about me wetting the sponge to apply the foundation, blotting the lipstick and giving me lessons on how to do this! I don't want that kind of work when I've got more important things to do like figure out the camera angle I want for a good portrait of someone I saw on the street.

Suddenly it dawned on me that Gail was simply trying to share with me something she loves. Her eyes get the same look that mine do when I'm talking to someone about photography or cookies and ice cream. It seems to be rare these days that you can find someone to share something you love to do or make or see. I realize I have many different kinds of friends that I can share my varied interests with. It is harder to find one person who is interested in all of the same things that I enjoy, but that's okay. I think you become too stagnant or set in your ways if you are sharing everything with only one person. With a variety of people, you get to see different aspects of the same things, often

...DNNSMLISE

aspects you would not have thought of. This revelation came to me when I told Gail, "Just you wait 'til I get you into my world of cameras!" But what's really nice is that we are willing to share our different interests with each other. It's okay if I don't drool over the announcement of a new line of products from the cosmetology scientists that promise no more wrinkles. Gail doesn't exactly get enthused about the latest color film with an ASA of 1000 that will hold flesh tones better.

Well I know when I'm licked, especially when threats of writing Gail up in the book don't work. I'm afraid I have to run now, I've got to make that dreaded trip to the make-up counter or find a new hiding place. Any suggestions!?

Too late! Gail caught me! I thought I had escaped because she wasn't able to meet me for lunch to pick up the appropriate products. Do you know she left a message on my answering machine at home asking me what was I doing that night? Hey, I know a trap when I hear one! Fortunately, I thought, I was already gone when she called. I spoke to her mother and asked her if she knew if Gail had gone for the make-up but she didn't know. Mrs. Hinton, that make-up was for me, Gail wasn't spending any more money on herself! Honest!

Well Gail made up my face for the reading and it was very nicely done. It met both of our approval — not too much for me and just enough for her! I thought I had gotten my revenge anyway because I wrote this chapter. I made the mistake of showing it to Gail before this book was published and now I have to add a footnote.

Before Gail even tried to convince me about make-up being good for the soul, she stressed the importance of good skin care. I was willing to listen to that portion of the conversation because I know I had neglected my face long enough. I agreed to try it, went to the demonstration (remember Gail, I went to two of them!) and even bought the recommended products.

DNNSMLISE...

Don't Need No Soaps, My Life Is Soap Enough!

And even more, I use them on a daily basis. Gail threatened to team up with Askari and Jamilah to get me if I didn't add this to the story. I started not to. "After all," I said, "It's my story, I can tell it anyway I want!" But then I remembered that God don't like ugly from anyone so I'm adding these last paragraphs. It's under protest but better safe than sorry. Besides Gail and my kids know where I live.

Sometimes You Just Have to Celebrate!

I have come to realize I have to be very careful because some times, (not very often) I can become very smug. Take this morning for example. I went to the Reading Terminal Market to get my breakfast. I knew exactly what I was going to get, some fruit. Well, now that I have lost that weight that belonged to somebody else, I just got full of myself. I passed between two aisles of wonderful goodies of cookies, cakes, pies, cannolis, candies of all description, and one of my favorites, cashew nuts. Did I even deviate from my direct path to the fruit stand? Of course not, I'm too smug knowing these goodies can't tempt me this morning! I smiled at the variety of cookies, I grinned at the cakes, and I almost laughed out loud at the cashews. "Oh, no you don't! I'm too strong for you guys! I know what you do to my waist, thighs and stomach. I'm having none of this! I eat right, I exercise, I am strong, I am good, and yes dare I say it, I'm disciplined and slim! How do you like that fellows? I'm laughing at your attempts to tempt me. HA! Go try your pitiful efforts on someone else!"

Then the "God don't like ugly" me kicked in. "Whoa girl friend, you better back that train up! It hasn't been that long since these goodies were not only in your hand, they were in

...DNNSMLISE

your mouth fighting for room as you stuffed more of them in!" I decided to get myself in order and stop trying to be so smug. I know I can easily be tempted and I'll confess, I did back up to take a long look at the carrot cake. Hey, they were mini cakes and I just wanted to see how that bakery made theirs as I'm planning on making my own this week-end. **Oops**, you didn't hear that, okay? Besides, this was in the A.M. If those goodies should show up on my door step around 10:00 P.M. when I'm trying to watch one of my favorite shows or a good movie, I'm a goner. The welcoming committee would have been in full session as I tried to decide which goodies were about to become my "bestest", long lost buddies. Let's see, I'll start with a couple dozen cookies, follow up with the chocolate covered whatever and finish up with the carrot cake and cashews!

But did this thought process really stop my smugness? **No!** I've spent too many months eating salads and passing on the fried chicken. Does one or two pieces of wing dings count? Hey it's not easy giving up your favorites even if it's for a good cause. In the meantime, I was too busy admiring my will power and the return of my real body to a smaller size. No I don't have to tell you what size I had gotten up to! Suffice to say, I'm slim again with determination and will power. What a deadly combination! Try it sometime and join me on a smug walk. It's a great feeling!

Allowance

Alright, here we go, this is from the book on parenting I've decided to write. It's the chapter entitled, "I don't care if I'm suffering from delusions, I've got a great idea". I have decided that I should receive an allowance from my children when I reach a certain age (that age is to be announced later). Hey, don't laugh, it's a great idea. Think about it, we have made major investments in them — education, values, clothing, home, etc. Don't you realize what we could have received from stocks if we had invested that much money with a brokerage firm? Why the money just from snacks alone would have been enough to guarantee us a new car every five years! Why the money we spent to help them keep up with the latest fashions should guarantee us a fabulous vacation every year!

Okay, I'll be the first to admit that my investment in my children is an investment in our future as African Americans and as human beings. I am sure my children will make their mark and contributions to the world. They have been raised to be good individuals with morals and principles. I know that was my job and my joy to make sure of that. And the bills that came from raising them were part of the package and the deal. Each of us will spoil our children in various ways and spend money on them that someone else would think is a waste. It gives us pleasure to do for our children and it should. We want to provide more for our children than our parents were able to provide for us. It is our way of honoring our parents and our ancestors for the scarifies they made.

However, I think the day should come that I get my paybacks. I don't mind collecting what's due me. I'm willing to settle for a small monthly sum. Call it my reward for a job well done. Remember, I worked hard to make my children self-reliant. That means they should be able to support themselves and have enough to give me my allowance. This is not the same money that is to be paid (perish the thought!) should they owe me for rent. No! That's inconceivable, it's not in my game plan, that they would owe me rent. Oh alright, I'll agree to the **Hypothetical** idea that they might not leave home. That means they are still living at home? Yeah, right, that's like Hollywood trying to tell us, "Remember, it's only a movie" as they scare us to death. Right! No, no, they will leave home! I do believe, I do believe!

Oh, alright, I'm willing to make a bargain. I won't demand an allowance if they don't come looking to me for money after they've earned their degree. I wouldn't want to hear that they can't move out because they paid me an allowance and now they're broke. I wouldn't want that on my conscience along with all the other guilt trips children try to put on you for doing your job as a parent/warden. Besides, my children will be in their own place thank you kindly! I do believe, I do believe. I've changed my mind — give me my allowance with interest!

Safe Repository for My Sanity

Things have gotten to the point that I need a safe repository for my sanity. It generally happens when people are trying to drive me insane. No one expects to be driven insane, it just happens. You think you are doing fine and the next thing you know, you're traveling on a fool's highway (see the poem following this chapter). Given that was the case, I thought it would be best if I could deposit my sanity somewhere safe. I thought about calling Frank Tyson up but I knew better than that. Frank has no patience for fools and would be too busy kicking my butt for not telling the fools off! That's the kind of friend he is and most times he's right. But the weak get weary. Even that statement holds no water with Frank, he won't allow me to call myself weak at any time!

I tried calling Juanita. I thought she would be a good keeper of sanity since she already is holding on to my "motherhood brownie points". Those are the points you get for the good things

Don't Need No Soaps, My Life Is Soap Enough!

you do as a mother. However, you lose points when you forget things like parent/teacher night at school, class trips the next morning when you forgot to buy groceries and the kids have to take lunch. Little things like that. Besides, Juanita loves to take points from me so she was more than willing to take on that job. But when I reached Juanita, she wondered if I had already lost my sanity since I was even considering her for the job. We have a tendency to check each other's sanity because the world can sure throw some mean things your way that make you wonder if there is any sanity in the world at all.

Well I guess the best thing for me to do is to hold on to my own sanity, at least for awhile. Besides, the way folks are losing their these days, they might volunteer so they'd have something to use to replace their own!

...DNNSMLISE

DNNSMLISE...   Bea Joyner

Traveling On A Fool's Highway

I finally came to realize, I was not traveling on my road.
For some reason, I kept finding myself
going down paths I had no business being on.
A Fool's Highway is full of twists, turns and deep, dark pits
that kept me covered in confusion and problems
and left me with a REAL BAD ATTITUDE!
I had made the decision to travel on my own road and I did
but because of various connections
those fools keep pulling me onto their highway
dealing with their nonsense that made no sense, except to them.
It didn't matter that they were the only ones
who thought it was sensible as long as they could keep me
traveling down a Fool's Highway.
But I discovered the reality is,
I only had to be on that road if I let them drag me there.
(Believe me, I would never have ventured on that
"Four Lane Highway To Insanity" on my own!)
So now I carefully watch for all warning signs
and verify all detour signs that take me off my road
'cause if you're not careful
you'll find yourself on a Fool's Highway
and never know how or when you arrived there.
It is important that you understand that no matter how you got there,
you can and must take yourself off it.
Just give yourself a reality check,
to see where and why you ended up there,
and get the hell off that Fool's Highway as quickly as you can
because the fools who put you there will try to make you think
you are crazy to want to be anywhere else!

Beatrice Joyner
6/7/95 1:55 P.M.
Copyrighted 1995

DNNSMLISE...

Don't Need No Soaps, My Life Is Soap Enough!

Who? Little Old Me? or...
The Chapter "The Girl Friends Club"
Has Threatened to Burn Because I Dared to Name Names!

Most of my life I have been told I am small, but I don't feel small. This is the same body I've had all of my life. With a few exceptions, like pregnancy and periods of added tonnage, I've always been close to the same size. I've never been six feet, three inches tall, so I don't know what it's like. I can't compare it to being five feet, three inches tall because it's all I've ever known. It doesn't seem small to me, it just seems like me. Every once in a while, I get a reality check that I am not very large. When I was in college, some of the men thought it was fun to carry me around the pool room like I was a baby doll or a toy. I'll admit, the first couple of times I thought it was fun. That didn't last long because the men seemed to feel they had found a new toy and anytime I walked in the pool room, someone thought they had to carry me around. Well, seeing that I know I'm not a baby, I had a tendency to get annoyed. I remember one brother picked me up and at the same time, I picked up a ruler and proceeded to rap his knuckles. Hey, I warned him not to do it, but perhaps because I'm small, he didn't think he had to listen. He found out otherwise and the others got the hint.

It's not that I can't see I'm small, I just forget that many others are taller and larger than me. I just don't think about it much, except at those times when my friends threaten to put me out of "The Girl Friends Club" and revoke my membership. For example, I called some of my friends up to tell them the good news (I thought it was!) that I had lost weight. I was so caught up in my own happiness of losing, that I forgot that

...DNNSMLISE

some of my friends were heading up the opposite end of the scale. One of them, yes it was Gail, called Celestine Wilson-Hughes up and they both proceeded to put me out of the club. It seems that my new weight was a dreaded reminder that they hadn't seen that number in many years and they didn't want to think about it. (This is when the threats came about burning this chapter!)

I only made matters worse when I proceeded to tell them that they weren't there when I was giving up fatty foods and eating salads. My self-control became a new reason for them to put me out the club. The fact that I eat cookies and ice cream and still maintain that dreaded number didn't endear me to their hearts either. In a separate episode that I didn't inform Gail or Celestine about, another member of the club was putting me out as well. I had also called Juanita with the good news of losing weight. She informed me that Dunkin' Donuts was having a $2 all you could eat day and she was willing to drive me there so I could regain my club membership for all the right reasons! I knew the threats were getting serious because Juanita doesn't know how to drive! I've had these kinds of threats before. When you work in an office environment, people have a tendency to look at each other's weight. Naturally that made me a candidate for some evil eyes. I even tried to join the office weight losing club but that didn't work. It seems I was the only one who didn't lose any weight and it didn't help that I was the smallest member of the club. No weight loss — out of the club!

Let me explain why my membership in "The Girl Friends Club" is so important to me. These women have my back in any kind of weather and they look out for me like its no body's business. They have put some restrictions on me but even I know that's for the best. For example, I have been strictly forbidden to go shoes, eye glasses or sunglasses shopping without a member of the club. Why? Because little ol' me has a tendency,

Don't Need No Soaps, My Life Is Soap Enough!

like Askari, to buy things too large for me. Notice I didn't say humongous. Celestine in particular has to pass approval on my shoes. Hey, when my feet hurt, looks are the least of my concerns. I bought some shoes but I had to take them to her for an inspection and they passed with the comment, "They look like Bea shoes." I'm not sure what that means but at least I wasn't ordered to take them back. I told hcr Jamilah had been with me and they had passed her inspection. Jamilah also made me put back a pair she described as too ugly. Remember my motto, if it's comfortable and reasonable priced, it's mine!

Nina took me shopping for sunglasses because she works close enough to me that we could go on our lunch hour. It was a good thing, because every pair I thought would work were deemed entirely too big. Juanita had a ball laughing at me when we went eyeglass shopping. I saw a pair of glasses that looked like they would fit. Just as I reached to pick them up, Juanita said very softly (so I would be the only one to hear her), "They look like something women wore in the fifties!" Boy, she sure knows how to hurt my feelings and no, I didn't touch them. I did pick up another pair that she laughed about because they said "Loonie Tunes" on them, but guess what? They fit. Later she told me she had her family falling out because unbeknown to me, I had picked up a pair of children's glasses. Hey, I told you I was small.

I thought that maybe if I shared something with my club members, I would be okay. I had received some panty hose in the mail that I didn't want - control top and control leg. They were a flashback to the days when my mother used to force me to wear a girdle. I decided a long time ago that I would never wear another girdle ever again in life. In those days, all mothers made you wear a girdle for fear that our shaking bodies might bring unwanted attention our way. Now how my mother managed to find one small enough to fit me, I have no idea. One of

...DNNSMLISE

my nicknames was "Splendid Splinter" so by rights I shouldn't have had to wear one. Unfortunately, it was part of the required armor that all "proper young ladies" had to wear. Now do you understand why I was trying to find a new home for those panty hose?

I started asking some women if they wanted them. The first question was always, "What size are they?" and I would answer, "Medium." That's when I discovered that many women are wearing Queen size panty hose mainly because the other sizes don't provide enough length or width. It's not that these women are particularly large, it's simply because the "charts" that are used to size the pantyhose were made up with "Twiggy" in mind. It's almost like those child development charts you find in the pediatrician's office. Most babies are far bigger and smarter than the charts say. Children are doing at three months what the charts say they shouldn't be doing until six or nine months. Obviously no one has updated the charts because they are no longer accurate. And the panty hose charts are worst. They make you feel like you're a blimp because the companies don't want to make sizes that fit real people. I doubt the store mannequins could wear anything smaller than large, just for height alone. So as you may have guessed, my club members were not amused that medium pantyhose were too large for me.

Then I got a reality check about my height. I've been used to looking up most of my life, but I didn't think that made me short. Askari has passed my height and loves to remind me of it every chance he gets. Well, he was supposed to pass my height, I've know since he was born that he would. He was much bigger at birth than I was, so I knew it was just a matter of time. Maybe I should explain why my height has never caused me much concern - my family is short. My parents were called "Big Al and Little Al" because they were both under five feet five. Okay, I'm stretching the truth. My mother is four feet, ten inches and my father was able to look down on the top of her head. I happened to be the tallest girl in my family. I was the one my mother would have reach up for things in the kitchen when she and I were cooking meals. It didn't matter to me that I had to climb up on a chair to get them, that was irrelevant. I was still the tallest!

Actually I think my girlfriends are really very proud of me for losing the weight but they just don't want to admit it. No, I'm not going to name names, those who support me might not want to risk losing their membership! Besides, the bottom line is not how tall you are or how much you weigh, the important thing is who you are on the inside. Right? I think everyone knows that's the truth, but I wouldn't recommend advancing that argument when my girlfriends are busy throwing me out of the club, one more time! How about the fast metabolism argument? Think that one will work? I'll let you know after I've been back in the club for a while. I'd hate to get thrown out when I've just been allowed back in!

...DNNSMLISE

DNNSMLISE... Bea Joyner

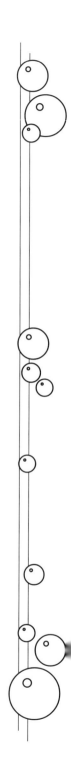

DNNSMLISE...

PART FOUR:

BEEN THERE, DONE THAT...
And Have the Life Experiences to Prove it!

Askari "Upon Attaining Manhood"

...DNNSMLISE

DNNSMLISE...   Bea Joyner

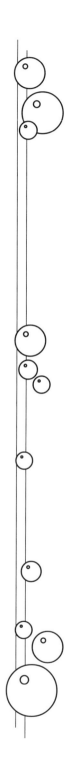

DNNSMLISE...

Card Carrying Member of the CRS Club
(If I Could Just Remember Where I Left it)

If genes truly do have anything to do with living a long life, I'm in pretty good shape. My father was eighty-five when he died and Mom is still going strong at eighty with relatively little physical health problems. My maternal grandfather also lived a long life.

One day I was talking to my mother and I mentioned some aches and pains. She started going on and on about how I was getting old and how your body starts falling apart at thirty. Now I am not one to get too concerned about reaching a certain age but thirty was one of them. I almost got depressed just thinking of it. Then a few years later Jamilah asked me how old I was. It was my birthday and I told her I would be thirty-five. She said "Wow, that's almost fifty years old." This was from a kid who at the time was having a hard time subtracting two from four. Of course I told her that was a few years away yet. She said "It's only fifteen more years." Mind you she wasn't fifteen at the time. She had me wondering if I should start looking into nursing homes for myself.

To make matters worse, my memory is failing. That's when I was introduced to the CRS Club. For those of you who don't know what that stands for it's "Can't Remember Stuff." It starts out with little things like where you placed your keys and moves on to bigger things like where in the parking lot you parked your car. And it gets progressively worse. You go into a room to get something, the next thing you know, you're in another room. You not only can't remember getting there, you have a hard time remembering why you wanted to be there. I quickly gave up getting headaches from trying to remember everyone's name

...DNNSMLISE

that I meet. I simply tell them I'm suffering from CRS. With some people, I don't even have to tell them what it means. That's when I know I'm speaking to a card carrying member. Once I tell those who don't know, I see that smile of understanding.

Of course, my children just see it as an opportunity to remind me that I'm getting old. So the battle is on. If they forget anything and can't remember it in a certain time period, I quickly tell them they're awfully young to be a member!

Pity Parties and Murphy's Law

The strangest thing happened to me. I found myself at a party I didn't ask to go to and wanted no part of. The party began in the waiting room of Philadelphia's Childrens Hospital. I had just been involved in another car accident and I was seeking treatment for Askari who had injured his arm. I didn't even realize the party had gotten started, I was too busy being miserable. I found myself saying, "I'm the world's worst driver! My insurance rates are going to skyrocket! My car is messed up all over again! How can I call the lawyer one more time about another accident?! What will he think of me?!" I looked so pitiful that the attending doctor took one look at me and told Askari, "Let's hurry up so we can get your mom some help." That's when I realized I was attending my very own, personal, don't need no help from anyone else to be pitiful Pity Party.

A Pity Party is when you can make yourself so miserable you don't need any help from your worst enemy 'cause you have done the job better than they ever could. You refuse all help to make things better because (excuse the cliché) you're as comfortable as a pig in mud. All you want is for everyone to agree with you and tell you how terrible life is treating you. And if they can show you different ways of how much more pitiful you are, you're in seventh heaven.

Pity Parties and Murphy seem to go hand in hand. Murphy is that Murphy from Murphy's Law — if something can go wrong, it will. Once something bad happens to you, the Pity Party begins and Murphy seems to be the only other guest! I had visions of trying to explain this one more accident to my attorney. It doesn't matter that the accidents weren't my fault. I could just imagine him rushing to the phone after I left to call the travel agent to say he didn't have to cancel that around the world cruise after all, I had just paid his way!

But somewhere in the back of my mind was this voice that was struggling to be heard. Each time I had two or three miserable thoughts, I could hear that voice say, "But you survived the accident and no one was seriously injured." Then there would be another miserable thought, "The damage to the car will cost thousands of dollars." But the voice said, "You've got good insurance coverage. Your deductible is only $500." Pretty soon I was listening to the voice and not the Pity Party. I had to remind myself as I do my children "Who said life is fair?"

By this time I decided the Pity Party was over. I started taking a realistic look at my situation and the first one was I wasn't dead. If I'm not dead, then anything is possible! Of course, Murphy and the Pity Party didn't want to leave, they were having too much fun. But their fun was all at my expense and I decided they were too expensive for me. I called a couple of my friends and dealt with my fears and concerns about the accident. Once I got the fears and concerns out into the open, it wasn't as bad as I thought. Yes, my car was damaged, but everyone was safe. As someone told me, I could always get another car. Yes, I would have to go back to the chiropractor but my body would recover. Yes, my insurance rates might go up but at least I had coverage.

...DNNSMLISE

DNNSMLISE...   *Bea Joyner*

I hate to admit it, but it seems I needed a reminder that bad things happen to everyone. It's easy to be positive when everything is going well, it's when things are bad that it's tough to be positive. Well I decided I'm tougher than Murphy and the Pity Party. I know they'll be back, ("That's life.") but maybe if I move and leave no forwarding address, they'll have a harder time finding me. Think I can confuse them? Maybe some make-up and a wig?

Gorilla Suits and Punk Status

I am not, by any stretch of anyone's imagination, a brave woman. I scare very easily and I claim "Punk Status" all the time. The reason I don't watch horror movies is because they scare me to death. There is a story in my family that when I was four, we got our first television. I am the youngest and I kept talking about being able to watch "Willie the Worm", some T.V. show character for children. This was long before "Barney". Well when we got the T.V., I was sat in front of it to see "Willie". The story goes that as soon as he came on, I ran screaming from the room scared to death.

The same sort of thing happened when the movie, "War of the Worlds" came out. My sister and I begged and pleaded with our father to take us. He finally agreed because he was such a big fan of Orison Wells and his original radio show which the movie was based on. We went to the movies and the story goes that when the titles came on, I got scared and started crying and screaming. I carried on so bad that we had to leave. My sister only got to see the titles and I don't know if she has ever forgiven me.

DNNSMLISE...

Don't Need No Soaps, My Life Is Soap Enough!

I wouldn't watch "Gremlins" until the movie was two or three years old and I had to watch it in the daylight hours! I have never watched "Psycho" and I have no intention of doing so. And anytime people try to pick with me about being a punk, I remind them of two things. Janet Leigh, the star of "Psycho" has never taken another shower since she made the movie. Stephen King, the king of horror stories sleeps with his lights on and his feet must be covered. Now I ask you, if these two are scared, is it any wonder that I am? I don't care if it's only a movie, it's too real for me. Believe me, the list of horror movies I have seen is very short. Anytime someone tries to drag me to see one, I claim "Punk Status". I am willing to show my feathers if anyone tries to call me a chicken. If proof is need, I'll even cluck like one.

Now horror is one thing, suspense is different. I have always loved shows like "Twightlight Zone" or "Alfred Hitchcock". If it makes you think and holds you in suspense, I'll watch it. And if you combine suspense with big time action scenes, you've got me. I had a hard time getting up my nerve to watch "Predator" and "The Terminator", however, I was right there to see "Terminator 2". It was great! I'm even planning to buy the "Terminator" videos. I even got brave and watched "Predator 2" all by myself at night!

I began to lose a little of my "Punk Status" when I went to college. Everyone would sit around at night watching all the classic horror movies on T.V. We would all pile into one room and scare ourselves to death. Suddenly I was brave! I could watch a Dracula movie without garlic and I could go to bed and sleep well! Then I was given the test. Everyone was going to the all night horror movie marathon. They all said I had to see "Night of the Living Dead". Okay, I'll do it! I'm badd! I'm brave! Let's go! Bring it on!

...DNNSMLISE

DNNSMLISE... *Bea Joyner*

The marathon was being held on Rutgers University's main campus. For some reason, I missed the bus and wound up going alone. I met up with some friends when I got there and we sat together. "Night of the Living Dead" was already in progress when we got inside. As I watched the people being eaten alive, being eaten dead and being eaten otherwise, I quickly accepted that I was not badd, I was not brave and I would never give up my "Punk Status" again if God would just let me survive!

I was intrigued with the movie because it was one of the few where the hero was a Black man with sense. He kept saving all those other dummies time after time. That was the only saving grace of the movie. But I was so scared and buried so deep in my chair, I didn't even know he had been killed. By the time the movie ended, it was too late to catch the bus back to my campus so I was stuck for the rest of the night watching horror movies. When I got back to my dorm, I tried to go to sleep. Unfortunately, my room was on the ground floor, and it overlooked a field. When I looked out, it was as if "Night of the Living Dead" was being filmed outside my window. It was all misty and I kept seeing the creatures coming after me. That cured me of trying to be brave! Well, God let me live, I didn't have a heart attack and I kept my promise! I have "Punk Status" for life!

There's one thing I don't understand about horror movies. It seems that the only people in the horror movies are really dumb ones. I mean why would anyone in their right mind go into a dark house when you know that's where the last fool was killed. Even without the music, I know something is up! Why don't they? I and my friends have shouted warnings for years at those fools but they just keep going into the dark. Don't they ever watch horror movies?! The only thing I can figure out is it's the scriptwriters' fault. Any reasonable and sensible person would be heading for the hills, but the script says, "Go into the house."

DNNSMLISE...

Don't Need No Soaps, My Life Is Soap Enough!

I guess that's why I'm not an actor. Me and that script writer would have to have a serious discussion about me going anywhere near those monsters. Also it helps to keep those neighborhoods reserved for certain folks. There's not many monsters showing up on street corners in the city. Who in their right mind would buy property that could hide monsters easily. If you don't believe me, go see Jack Nicholson in "Wolf"!

My "Punk Status" is not just for movies, I use it whenever I get scared of anything. I've claimed it when relationships didn't seem be going the way I thought they should or I thought the person was out of my league. I've claimed it when I didn't want to do certain jobs. I've wanted to claim it many times when being a mother is difficult but I can't. The one thing I have learned is that it's dangerous to push someone who is scared too far. There are many people who will jump badd at the drop of a hat, that's not the one to watch out for. It's the quiet, shy person who gets pushed too far that you have to be extremely careful of.

I can only be pushed so far and it takes a lot to get me to that point. It's what I call "The Gorilla Suit" situation. Everyone knows that gorillas are badd and you better not mess with them. Some people keep their gorilla suit on all the time. I don't. I don't like to live like that but if you get me to the point that I have to reach for my gorilla suit to deal with you- **Watch Out!** First of all, I'm going to be pissed that you got me to that point. Second, since I don't own a gorilla suit, you have caused me to have to go rent one. If you've forced me to rent one, you're in serious trouble because you've made me as the kids say "have to go there" or get to that "Level". I become seven feet tall, 500 pounds and **Mean!** You don't want to mess with me when I'm in that state of mind. It doesn't happen often but it can happen. I have sent men running with just one glance when I'm in that state of mind. I've seen people make a wide path around me because they recognize what is happening.

...DNNSMLISE

Fortunately, this doesn't happen very often and I can have the suit cleaned and put back in storage until it's needed again. And I'm glad 'cause I don't like being the person I become when I have that suit on. Maybe I'm going at this in the wrong way, maybe I should rent that suit to go to the movies in. Nah! I'd still be scared and it's too hot inside that suit to be sweating the way I would!

Don't Want to Look Like I'm Confused

I never, in my wildest dreams, imagined that one day I would be a prude. I mean I wore mini skirts so short, my "pea coat" was longer. I can remember defending myself to some older women that short skirts did not a hussy make. I think becoming a prude is a rites of passage to old age. Of course nobody bothers to tell you this. It's sort of like that lost real training manual on how to be a parent. No one wants to tell you the truth for fear that you won't want to do it.

It seems the older I get, the more I disagree with the latest fashions. I remember hot pants. I also remember I wasn't allowed to wear them. Now it seems it's a style called "Dazy Dukes" shorts. I know I'm telling my age but I remember a comic character named "Daisy" from the "Little Abner" comic strip. She wore these "disgraceful" shorts (according to the old folks) about the same length. Then there was the "Dukes of Hazards" show with a "Daisy" character who also wore those shorts. My description of those shorts are panties with fringe. I just don't think it's something that you should parade around the streets in. I know — I'm a prude.

Don't Need No Soaps, My Life Is Soap Enough!

I think the problem is most of these young ladies parading around in their "Daisy Dukes" aren't built like the aforementioned "Daisy". I know I thought that was the case with the old ladies I argued with. They were just upset because I looked good (so I thought) in my mini skirts. Their bodies would not have looked the same in mini skirts that I did. That's why they were so upset. I just didn't see the same thing in my mirror when I got dressed that they saw.

I went to an after work party a couple of years ago. I wandered into the ladies room where the young ladies were trying to pull down their dress or top to show more cleavage. That's when I realized, I was too old for the crowd. This was at the time of the Ray Charles commercial, "You've got the right one, baby!" When two young ladies showed up in dresses trying to imitate the ones in the commercial, I knew it was time to leave. Their sequins were the size of quarters and they were not the "right ones, baby." I already warned you I was a prude.

And that's another thing. Why doesn't Nature give you the body you want when you need it. I mean I was called "Splendid Splinter" when I was growing up. I wouldn't mind having some of that slenderness now that the fat demons are on my doorstep. But Nature doesn't seem to think that way. Those fat demons would take up permanent residence if I didn't have the will power (Ha!) I do about eating cookies and ice cream. I read a piece on what the world would be like if the life cycle was reversed. That means I could have a body to die for just before I died. I guess Nature knows what it's doing, I'd probably kill myself off too soon if I looked like that. I've always thought if I could just look as good as Lena Horne now, let alone when I'm her age, I'd be happy!

What I don't understand is why manufacturers are willing to sell Spandex in sizes too large for the material. A friend told

...DNNSMLISE

me she doesn't want to look as if she's confused by wearing these so called fashions. I agree. I just don't think showing off my body with fashions designed for teenagers is a good idea. I might feel differently if I had a body like Tina Turner but I don't. Some women look like they've been caught up in a time warp and refuse to let go of the fashions that looked good on them when they were younger. I heard of a number of daytime talk shows where the daughters were complaining about their mothers dressing like teenage hussies and from what I saw, they didn't have the body or a youthful face to go with it. They just looked like they were confused about who they are. I know, I'm a prude.

Well, I guess I might as well accept that I am a certified prude. The fashion moguls and I don't agree on too many things but as long as they sell pants and skirts that cover my knees, I'll keep buying and clucking like those old ladies I remember when I was growing up. "Hey, young girl, where's the rest of your dress?" Oh no, I really am old!

Listening to that Voice of Reason

There are times when someone will speak to me with a voice of reason. Unfortunately, I'm not always ready to listen. In fact, I usually try to get that voice to change to my reasoning because my reasoning makes perfect sense to me. And usually my reasoning **only** makes sense to me. But do I care?! Of course not! However, I have to remember to get out of my self-righteous indignation state of mind and listen. Why? Because that voice is usually right.

Lately that voice of reason is coming from Askari. I have a hard time dealing with/remembering that there is a man in my household. He doesn't pay bills yet, and he doesn't contribute to the rent money but I still have a man in my household. He is a young man, as I have to keep reminding him, but still there is a man in my household. And that little boy, excuse me, young man can speak with wisdom at times.

I had gotten dressed one morning and was putting on some lip gloss. "I don't know why you would want to put that cat pee on your lips." was his comment. Now you know I had to ask him what he was talking about. It seems he had seen a science program on T.V. that said women's make-up is made from cat pee. Now I have to admit that Askari loves those kinds of shows and he pays close attention to them. But I just can't imagine there being a factory in America where they line up cats to "milk" them or collect their pee. Can you imagine the smell?!

Of course I dismissed his comment as Askari nonsense but Askari was having none of that this particular morning. "I don't know why you women do those things to yourself. You put all that junk on your face. No man wants to kiss a woman with cat pee on her face." Well seeing as I am not kissing anyone these days except my kids on the cheeks, I didn't think that was a problem. Neither did he because he did allow me to kiss him that morning. Besides, I politely told him I couldn't wait until he gets a girlfriend who wears plenty of make-up. Of course he told me he won't have a girlfriend who wears lots of make-up. Ha! You know I'm waiting for that day (years from now of course, according to my game plan) when some young lady charms Askari and he is deep in the thralls of her magic because I'm going to be the first one to remind him about that cat pee if Jamilah doesn't beat me to the punch.

But make-up isn't the extent of his "wisdom". I broke a nail one day down to the fleshy part and I was trying to bandage it and take care of the bleeding. Who should wander my way but Askari. "I don't know why you women grow your nails so long anyway. All they do is break off and then you complain about the pain. Why don't you just keep them short?" Need I tell you I was in no mood for that voice of reason at that moment. I was too busy trying to figure out how to cut the nail to end some of the pain and maintain a pretty nail too. "Men don't like long nails anyway," Askari had to add. Now, I have heard many a man talk about their desire to have a woman with long red nails glide them down his back. I've even heard of men proudly discussing the wounds those nails can inflict at the proper moment. Of course, I know he is still a young man and I don't know if I really am ready to hear Askari getting into those kinds of conversations. There are some things that a mother really doesn't want to hear from her son. This time I didn't even respond. The pain had all of my attention and I didn't want to give him any new avenues to try to explore.

Finally I had to listen to him discuss my high heels. I usually will wear a comfortable pair of shoes or sneakers to work and carry the heels I want to wear that day. It does mean extra weight in my brief case, but I don't mind. But Mr. Askari does. "I don't know why you women wear high heels anyway. You should just wear flats or something comfortable. You just hurt your feet, grow corns, and complain." Now really, do I need to hear this as I'm rushing out in the morning trying to find the most comfortable pair of heels that will match my outfit when I'm already twenty minutes behind schedule?

But as much as I hate to admit it, he's right. Of course I haven't admitted this to him yet. I'm too busy buying heels that promise comfort — Life Stride, Naturalizers, Easy Spirit or any other brand that looks like they may keep their promises. I have a real appreciation of Pearl Bailey now. I use to watch her on T.V. and she was known to pull off her heels and say "Honey, my feet hurt!" She was a classy lady who knew how to dress well and always had gorgeous heels on. She also knew when enough was enough and she pulled them off when she couldn't stand them anymore. Of course none of this makes sense to that voice of reason named Askari. He doesn't think it makes sense to pull off shoes, he thinks they shouldn't be put on at all if they are going to hurt.

I might be more inclined to listen to that voice of reason named Askari if I spent hours putting on make-up, constantly went to the nail salon or wore nine inch heels but I don't. Of course that voice of reason doesn't care how much of these things I do, the degree to which I indulge in these things is irrelevant to him. He's even threatened not to take care of me in my old age if I continue along this path. Do I listen to that voice of reason named Askari? Of course not, I just remind him he owes me for all the diapers I changed. Good reasoning right? No! So slowly I am keeping my nails shorter, my lipstick less and my heels lower. After all, I may not want to listen to Askari, but that voice of pain is hard to ignore.

Going Shopping Part 2:
Fashions and Other Related Topics

This is another page from the Real Parent Training Manual. It's found in the section called, "My child is a teenager and I am now consided really old." It's also known as "Mom, we've switched roles, I am now the parent!"

Askari has reached that point in life when he has decided he has to help me with my fashions and this includes hair style. I decided to go back to wearing a natural after having let my hair grow. I had been wearing one plait in the back and curled the front and this was acceptable to Mr. Askari. Perhaps I should have warned him when I decided to get it cut, but hey, who's the parent here? When I came back from the barber shop, I thought Mr. Askari was going to faint. My hair is very soft so the hair cut looked like a buzz cut. He sat me down on the couch, put his arms around me and said very excitedly, "Mom, you can't do this, you're messing with my image!" He kept telling me I needed to get a perm or if I insisted on keeping a natural, it wasn't short enough and I needed to get it cut in a box style. I refused, and as I reminded him, I never said he was messing with my image when he was running around with a dirty diaper and had a snotty nose. But I forgot who I was dealing with. I really forgot when I came home and told him I had gotten compliments on my hair style. Askari looked me dead in my eyes and said, "Yeah, I'll bet the person was old!" You know he was right.

Next came my baseball cap. I had gotten a very nice African print baseball cap but the material wasn't the problem. "Mom, the cap has no shape!" Askari was speaking about the brim. So while we were at the store getting some items for him, I looked at some caps. Askari found a cap that he liked but the band was broke. I thought the cap was nice too. I told him to look in the stack for another one but he and his buddy were too busy trying to fix it. I looked in the stack and found one for me. Of course Askari thought it was his. I politely told him it was not. "Mom that's not right!", was his comment. Hey, he didn't want to do the looking, therefore I had my cap, he still had to look for his. However, the prices were reasonable enough that we both got three or four. I thought, now I'm back in Askari's good fashion graces. Unfortunately I soon lost it.

At the time of this writing, the latest fashion craze for young men is plaid shorts. I don't mind plaids but these are some of the ugliest plaids I had seen outside of a golf course. As he and his buddy excitedly dug through the shorts trying to match them up to shirts (thank God, the shirts were solids!), I couldn't hold back the laughter any longer. "You've got to be kidding me,

Don't Need No Soaps, My Life Is Soap Enough!

those shorts are too ugly!" That was the moment I stopped being in Askari's good fashion grace. "Mom, these are happening!" I can't wait to take some good color photographs of Askari in those shorts so years later, his children and I can sit around and have a good laugh.

Now I have a plaid pants suit that I am really pleased about because I have lost enough weight to take it out of the section of clothes we all have. It's that delusional, mirage section of our closet of clothes that don't fit anymore, will probably never fit anymore but we love them too much to give them away. Fortunately for me, not only can I wear those clothes, some of them are quite comfortable. (Hey Eric Bonner, the personal trainer, thank you, thank you, thank you!) Mr. Askari doesn't think there is any need for celebration. "Mom, you've got to be kidding! That suit is smoked!" Now, for those of you who need an interpretation of the term "smoked", here it is. "Smoked" means not good. That's it, that's as much as I was able to comprehend. The best I can tell you, as with most of these kids terms, it's something that meets the kid's approval or it doesn't. I don't have time to sign up for their language class. Besides, give it a couple of weeks and it will be too old to use, unless you don't want to appear hip. Wait a minute, I don't think you can use the word "hip" unless you don't mind appearing truly ancient.

And let us not forget the "Hey, it's not as bad as what others are doing" argument. Even Jamilah has gone that route. She came home on break from college with a second set of holes in her ears. When I asked her about it, she just started telling me how much different stores tried to charge her to pierce her ears and ignored the part about my concern of more holes. Instead she said, "The other kids have holes in their nose, stomach and/or nipples!" It's amazing how well that argument works. You wind up shaking your head saying," Well, it could be a whole lot worst!"

...DNNSMLISE

Then of course, there's the, "Mom you have to do it because everyone else is!" argument. Of course Askari tried to take this to the extreme. He wanted to know what I was going to get him for his eighth grade graduation. I figured since I paid the tuition bills all these years, a kiss should be enough. I thought the brother was going to pass out! "Mom, some of the kids are getting two thousand dollars!" (Askari, a word to the wise, don't go to the far extreme when trying to reason with me.) I politely told him he should go live in that person's house 'cause that ain't happening here. As I told him, I'm preparing him for life, that money could be better used for college. Of course when you're in the thralls of "everyone else is doing it", that statement is never even heard.

The only thing I hope is, this too shall pass. Jamilah and Askari will continue to be reminded by me that I am the parent. And someday, if I'm lucky, I'll be around to see their children try to make them seem ancient. By that time, my grandchild will probably think I'm pretty cool because to really get my revenge on Jamilah and Askari, I'll have to sit in my rocker and say, "Leave that child alone and get him/her what they want!"

Believe Me, I'm No Expert on Love

Some of you may be wondering why there aren't any chapters about romance and dating. That's because there isn't any romance or dating in my life right now. Besides, I seem to do it so badly, I think I should write a book about how not to date. I started writing one because I thought I was having such bad luck in getting one of those good guys in my life that I decided I could at least warn other women about what not to do in a relationship.

DNNSMLISE...

Don't Need No Soaps, My Life Is Soap Enough!

Things like —

When you meet someone whom you are interested in and he asks for your home phone number, make sure he gives you his home phone number. If he hesitates or doesn't want to give it to you, you can be pretty sure a jealous female resides in that household. You can bank on it that it's not his grandmother, mother, aunt, cousin or sister.

Let me give you an example of why I'm not an expert on love. One day my buddy Ted found me wandering the streets muttering and cursing under my breath. Of course he had to stop me because that's not my "modus operandi". Especially since I walked right past him and never even looked at him. He took one look in my eyes and said, "What's wrong?" I nearly began speaking in tongues I was so angry. "That man called me last night at 3:00 A.M. wanting to know if he could come over when I haven't seen or heard from him in days! You know I was going to hang up on him, but he wanted to keep me talking on the phone! Do you know what he said? How are my children? At 3:00 A.M.!" Believe me, it's days like this that make me want to seriously consider buying that gorilla suit!

Well as you can see, this was a very one-sided conversation. Poor Ted couldn't have gotten a word in sideways, edgewise or any other kind of way that day. Ted knows me well enough to know that it was best to just let me ramble. And in case you're wondering, no that man did not come over. I heard Sonia Sanchez call this kind of situation, "Loving on an installment plan." One female comedian put it more succinctly as "F—ing on a lay-away plan!" Basically these types of men aren't serious about anything more than a quick shot.

Now don't get me wrong, men aren't the only ones with hormone problems. As I've told my children, sex can be the most wonderful experience in the world or it can be the ugliest and I've had both. I've learned the hard way to choose wisely

...DNNSMLISE

with the top of my head, not with the lower middle part of my body. Unfortunately, too many people use that latter body part to make important decisions. I tell people I missed out on the "Sexual Revolution" because I was so in love with one man I couldn't see anyone else. By the time I left him, the AIDS epidemic had begun and I'm sorry, I don't think a shot is worth dying for.

I'll be the first to admit that I'm embarrassed to make that trip to the drug store but I think it's important that someone makes that trip. I had an experience where the heat was on and it wasn't until the last moment I realized he hadn't made that trip. Honey, I made *us* get out of bed and I drove him to the drug store. I waited in the car while he made the purchase. I know he thought I was insane 'cause I kept giggling. Hey, this mandatory need for condoms was a new experience for me but it wasn't one I was willing to put my life on the line for. Needless to say, the feeling was gone and I haven't heard from that brother since. The old folks keep telling us to be prepared but I obviously wasn't listening *again*.

Now I have my male buddies on special alert should the occasion arise again. They have to go to the store for me and we've already agreed that I have to give them plenty of notice. Of course, you know they have great fun at my expense. Ted and Stanley Wilson Jr. have brought me coupons from "Condom Nation", a store in Philadelphia. You can tell from the name what their specialty is. In fact, Stan had the nerve to proudly announce to me quite loudly in the lobby of the building in which I work, that a company had just put the extra large size condom in the stores because as he gleefully reminded me "One size does not fit all!" Or my other buddy who told me he'd be glad to purchase them as long as he was allowed to test them out with me first. Of course the answer is no because he is a friend, not a lover, so he threatened to put holes in them. You know he's off my stand-by list!

I have been fortunate in my life to have good male friends and that's very important to me. In fact, my friendships have lasted far longer than my loverships. I think that's because these friends and I are more willing to work at the relationship than the lovers were. These men have been my friends, my protectors, my consolers, my confidants, my "Girl, I'll kick your butt if you don't straighten out!", my "Let's go to the movies" buddies. We enjoy, understand, and accept each other's strengths and weaknesses.

They've helped me understand other men better. Case in point — there was a man whom I had met but we weren't really getting along. I felt it best to part company but he seemed to want to continue. I couldn't understand why so I asked Stan. Stan said very calmly, "That's probably because you've worked a 'Mo Better' on him." I had no idea what he meant but he was very patient with me to make sure I understood. Stan knows once I've made a mistake, I try not to repeat it. It finally dawned on me that the brother was only interested in one part of me. That kind of information prevented me from getting involved with men who didn't have my best interest at heart.

All I can tell you about love is to be careful. I still believe and know there are good guys out there but there are bad ones too. So in case you keep running into the bad ones, I've included the following two poems. They've kept me out of a lot of bad situations and if you're interested in getting your membership card for "Fools Anonymous", please feel free to contact me.

...DNNSMLISE

DNNSMLISE...   Bea Joyner
"Fools Anonymous"

This is a personal plea for help.
I am directing this to any member of the F.A.
Formally known as "Fools Anonymous".
I am in danger of slipping off the wagon
and becoming a fool for "that" man.
I don't need anyone to identify my situation
or even put it in perspective.
I can do that for you.
I am lonely, having been without love for some time now
and "that" man has walked into my life and somehow, someway
been able to reach deep inside and touch my heart.
At first he was very careful with it showing great sensitivity
and little by little he widened the space
both to let himself in and to let my heart out.
Fortunately, I was careful not to let him in completely
or my heart out all the way.
If I had there would be no reason to call the F.A.
I would have been gone completely.
But now he has exposed what I am afraid might be his true self.
I find myself in danger of not being willing to accept what I see,
but is so obvious to anyone else.
The problem is that I think what I was feeling was really real
and this love was and is
all that I have been waiting so long for
and all these other "real" incidents
are just figments of my imagination.
So I'm calling out for a F.A. member to come help me,
only a reformed fool will understand what I'm saying.
Because if I don't get some help quick,
I will be getting fittings for a ring in my nose,
a noose on my neck
and a broken heart.

Beatrice Joyner
12/12/86 11:50 A.M.
Copyrighted 1989

DNNSMLISE...

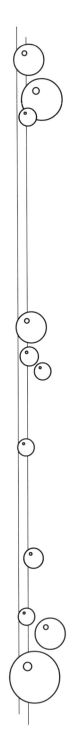

Don't Need No Soaps, My Life Is Soap Enough!

Four Questions

Don't think that your willingness to deal with my body
means you can deal with all of me.
Unless you are prepared to deal with all of me,
you won't have the opportunity to deal with my body.
I am seeking someone who is capable of handling my strengths
as well as my weaknesses.
I know I have frightened men away because of my strengths
but I am seeking my equal, not just a bed partner.
For those of you who think you can handle me
simply because I am petite in size,
you must answer four questions
and I ask that you carefully consider the questions before you answer.

#1. Are you married?
#2. Can you stay the whole night?
#3. Can you take phone calls in the middle of the night?
#4. Are you going to stay around to help me wash and fold up sheets?

Question #1 is important 'cause I don't do marrieds.
Question #2 means are you willing to spend some time with me
or are you just looking for a one night stand?
Question #3 means when I need you will you be there for me?
Question #4 means are you willing to be involved in a real relationship,
a long term relationship and all that goes with it
'cause it's hard to fold up king size sheets by yourself.

Don't make the mistake of considering me a lightweight
because of my size.
Take a full and true measurement of me
before you hitch up your pants and say
"I can handle that!"

Beatrice Joyner
10/20/88 3:15 A.M.
Copyrighted 1986

...DNNSMLISE

I'm a Dragon Slayer

Fear is a very powerful motivator. I find, like many others, I am very fearful at times. There are two things I've learned about fear. It can keep you in your place without anyone guarding you to make sure you stay in your place. You'll become your own jailer. You'll chastise and beat your own self up if you dare to move out of place. OR as I said before, it can cause you to become a five hundred pound gorilla. You have to decide what fear will have you do.

Although I have stated I'll claim punk status, I can operate like I'm that five hundred pound gorilla. This is usually not a conscious decision, I just have too much to do to be sitting around in place. I've trained managers and supervisors for the City of Philadelphia. One day my manager stepped into my classroom to give me some information. The class was almost ready to start when one of the participants tried to sneak out to grab a cup of coffee. I paused from what I was saying to my manager and very politely told that man, "Get back in here!" and finished what I was saying to my manager. My manager looked at me in amazement and said, "How did you do that?" "Do what?", I asked. Then I looked at the participant. He was a man about 6' 3" and I had stopped him dead in his tracks. Hey, I had things to do! It was time to start the class and he would have delayed and disrupted it if I hadn't called him back. Later I found out the man was a prison guard supervisor with about 10 years experience of being a guard himself. Hey, I didn't care, I had things to do.

Unfortunately, there are times when the other kind of fear takes over and without realizing it, I have marched myself into a corner, put handcuffs on and dared myself to move. I usually

Don't Need No Soaps, My Life Is Soap Enough!

find myself in that corner without consciously knowing how I got there. I was in the process of preparing myself for another court session on the custody of Jamilah and Askari. I was gathering up my papers when I discovered myself in the corner. I didn't even realize my self-talk had started. I began to experience cold sweats as I imagined the court deciding to take my children away from me or how the need might arise again for me to file protection papers.

"WHOA!", I told myself. "You've come too far to go that route." I began to review all of my accomplishments. I have a very good job as the result of a promotion. I've given photographic exhibits and have received good reviews from curators and critics. I'm a good mother and have done well by my children. Pretty soon, I was out of that corner and into my gorilla suit. Sometimes you have to put on your gorilla suit and get with *yourself* to get *you* in order!

Well, that's when I wrote the poem "Dragon Slayer". Now anytime I feel myself being led off to that corner, I whip out this poem and get busy. Hey, I've got too much to do to be sitting in a corner somewhere!

...DNNSMLISE

Dragon Slayer

It is important to me to remember,
I have to be my own dragon slayer.
It would be nice to wait for some knight to ride down the hill
and do the deed for me
but the reality is, knights on hills are rare
and dragons are quite commonplace.
I have to get busy and slay whatever dragon comes my way
or crosses my path with evil intentions.
I could be dead and buried in my grave
or deep in the pit of the dragon's belly
before that knight ever showed up.
So please excuse me while I hike up my skirts
and sharpen my sword.
I have to let those dragons know,
they're messing with the WRONG princess!

Beatrice Joyner
4/10/95 10:00 A.M.
Copyrighted 1995

Don't Need No Soaps, My Life Is Soap Enough!

While You're Climbing That Mountain, Be Sure to Check Where You've Been

I have a tendency to admire a lot of people. They're prettier than me, more intelligent, more talented, etc. As I strive to become better at what I do, I keep them in mind as an example of a goal to obtain. I tell them, I want to be just like them when I grow up! What I have discovered is that while I'm doing that, I don't take the time to appreciate my own talents and accomplishments.

I had a reminder of this recently. It was a holiday and Jamilah, Askari and I were trying to get our plans together. Jamilah wanted to spend time with her boy friend so I was going to take Askari to the movies. I felt bad because I knew they wouldn't have barbecue for dinner because it's not a good idea to try to set up a charcoal grill in an apartment and we hadn't been invited to a cook-out. I began to feel sorry for my children because they aren't in a two parent family, they weren't going to have barbecue for dinner, so what kind of mother was I? I even let Askari run a guilt trip on me. I wanted to take him to see a movie but he wasn't interested in the movie I chose. "I'd rather stay at home." Right! Now not only isn't he in a two parent family, is getting no barbecue, he'd rather stay home. So I agreed to take him to see "Judge Dredd." Now usually "R" rated movies are on my off-limits list for Askari, but the guilt was stronger that day. After all he's only going to be young once, he'll soon rather spend time with his "boys" than his mom, etc. (I've noticed when I'm in this state of mind, I get a lot of etc.'s!) And as if that wasn't enough, I dropped him back off at home when the movie was over and went to see the movie I had wanted to see at first.

...DNNSMLISE

And to add injury to insult, I left orders for Jamilah to fry the chicken as soon as she got in.

As I was driving to the movie theater, the guilts were going on strong and I started thinking about my girl friends who are married and would be spending a typical family holiday. But I also started remembering the realities of their situations. They don't have the freedom to go to the movies like I was on my way to do. Their children give them the same grief that mine give me. Their husbands aren't always as easy to get along with as it may appear or as supportive as they would like them to be. I've learned a long time ago that when you put two adults together, even in a very loving relationship, you still have two personalities to deal with. That ain't easy to do all the time. Plus these women rarely get a free moment to themselves without the children or husband interrupting.

I decide to take stock of my accomplishments. No I don't have a house but I have a nice apartment. If anything goes wrong with anything in it, I simply call the building manager. I don't have to cajole some man into finally getting around to fixing anything. No, my kids don't live in a two parent household, but they are healthy, intelligent children. No, I don't have a husband, but I can come and go as I please, provided that I have taken care of Jamilah and Askari first. No, I don't have a male supporting me financially or spiritually, but I don't have to put up with bills being created that I don't know about or are not being paid or naysayers. And once I close my door at night and Jamilah and Askari are in bed, my time is all my own. All of the guilt didn't disappear, but I thoroughly enjoyed that movie. And Jamilah can cook some mean fried chicken!

So what did I learn? To celebrate me for what I've already accomplished. Not to worry about Jamilah and Askari, they are turning out to be (as I knew from the moment they were born) two beautiful children. And not to be so busy looking up the mountain that I forget to look back and celebrate how far I've already climbed!

I Refuse to Waste Good Energy on a Negative Situation

I found myself in a situation that I'm sure millions of others have. I was suddenly person non gratis at my job. I had seen this process before but I had never experienced it myself. When organizations clean house, re-organize, re-engineer, down size, right size or whatever the term of the day is, there are those that are in and those that are out. Just call them "Innies" and "Outies." Being an "Outie" can change your whole life, especially if you are living from paycheck to paycheck. I realize that's what organizations count on. Unless you are independently wealthy or Ed McMahon showed up at your door instead of mine, you need the job to provide your food and shelter. If you are independently wealthy you would probably just flip the organization some obscene gesture when the layoff notice arrived. If you aren't rich, the layoff notice becomes the center of your life. When your food and shelter are threatened, it is difficult to concentrate on anything else. You revert (according to the Maslow Hierarchy of Needs), from Self-Actualization (the desire to be the best you can be for yourself) to Basic needs (how the hell do I pay the bills that were barely being covered by my pay check to covering those same bills with no check?) Forgive me, but obscenities suddenly enter your life as well. Trust me, I was deep in a negative situation.

The reality was, it was my wake-up call. I had been relatively safe because I am a good employee. I knew the slide to obscurity was a very fast one, so to protect myself, I went back to school to increase my skills. I knew that an additional degree

...DNNSMLISE

was no guarantee to prevent being laid off, but it would make me more marketable. The reality of how fast your world can change was suddenly mine. I decided the main thing I had to focus on was me. Even if I found myself an "Outie", there were certain realities that still remained. I could breath, my legs worked and my brain was having only a temporary setback. The key for me was to keep focusing my energy on positive things not the negatives.

Yeah right, that sounds real good. Let's all get together and hum, light a candle and gaze into our crystals and all of this will disappear. But believe it or not, it is simply a matter of you making up your mind that the negative forces don't control you. It doesn't mean you suddenly find yourself back as an "Innie." It means you have <u>begun</u> to change the situation by changing your thinking. I was not foolish enough to think I could tell everyone involved in changing my world from being an "Innie" to being an "Outie", that they could go to hell and remain employed. What it did mean for me was I had to concentrate and focus on me, not the negative situation. By putting myself in that frame of mind, the powers that be began to re-align to allow me some breathing room. It came in small ways, like people showing support for me or giving me words of encouragement. These people couldn't change my situation but I could add their positive energy to mine and become just a little stronger.

At this point I have no idea how this scenario will end. I might be hitting that massive line of unemployment. What I discovered was by refusing to surrender all my energy to something negative, something positive came my way. I may still have to change careers, or take a major cut in pay. But I learned I had more control over the situation than the negative forces believed. There are only twenty-four hours in a day, seven days in a week and a certain period of time allotted to each of us in life. And as far as I can tell, you don't get a chance to say,

DNNSMLISE...

Don't Need No Soaps, My Life Is Soap Enough!

"Oops, I'm sorry. Let me try that all over again." If you waste your positive energy, it's gone. You may realize the error of your ways and correct your course, but you can't grab back your yesterdays.

I decided not to waste my positive energy. It didn't make the nervous stomach go away, but it prevented it from lasting as long. But just to be on the safe side I tried to borrow someone else's crystal but they needed as much as I did. Instead, I constantly chanted to myself to keep the negative forces at bay. I repeatedly told myself, "Sister get yourself in gear, you've got work to do if you want to get out of here." I remained conscious of my bills because I know that bills are a fact of life. Bills will be there long after I've gone. But I don't have to waste my positive energy on someone else's negativity. Every small step that takes you out of a negative situation means one less step in the mess. But hey, in the mean time, brother, can you spare a candle? How about that crystal?

Wanted: Female Engineer Willing and Able to Design

This is one time I freely admit I am being sexist and I really don't care. This is too important to me not to be. I think you will understand my feelings when I tell you I have just received my yearly mammogram. I know anyone who has ever been squeezed in that device will agree with me that it could only have been designed by a **Man**. Is that being sexist? You try being squeezed in a vice that does not allow you to breath, let alone move and tell me that a woman designed it. No woman in her right mind would **Ever** design a machine that takes your breast, (no matter how big or small) and try to mash it to a piece of flesh that can't be more than one inch high. If

...DNNSMLISE

that isn't bad enough, the machine is **Ice Cold**! And to make matters even worst, the technician insists you have to press close to the ice cold machine with your naked body, as if it was the best lover you ever had! The machine is cold enough that I started formulating in my mind a plan to take care of the freezer burn I was sure it would leave. I could only pray that the machine didn't take any of my skin with it as well. Perhaps like me, you've had at least one technician who tried to tell you it doesn't hurt or you were just being a baby. Was this a case of adding insult to injury, or a test to determine if you really have much self control?

I think it is for the protection of the male species that these technicians are female. As you can imagine, there is the privacy issue of exposing your naked breast to a male you might never see again in life. He wouldn't have to worry about having a nice day. Instead, he would have to wonder how to survive the wrath of millions of women who don't appreciate being squeezed flat as a pancake, (if the technician is feeling generous that day!). I don't think Denzel Washington or Fabio (or any other hunk whose name you would care to substitute) would escape with their lives after putting a woman through that torture! I believe the only man who might have the slightest understanding of what I am talking about is the actor, who played in the comedy, "Love and Hate." There was one episode when he had to get a mammogram because a mass had been detected in his breast. Suddenly I could gleefully laugh out loud at having a man placed in the same machine women, over a certain age, are expected to visit once a year. It is always amazing to women to see a man cry at the slightest example of pain we suffer as a normal course of business. Suddenly that dreaded machine was delivering to a man, any man, the pain we suffered. I have to admit, I was certain I could get him to join me in the hunt for a new designer.

Don't Need No Soaps, My Life Is Soap Enough!

Please don't misunderstand me. I am eternally grateful that the mammogram was invented. It has saved millions of lives and breasts by being able to detect masses, some that often are too small to be felt in routine breast examinations. I will willingly submit myself to this torture every year, knowing that without it, I might suffer the painful devastations of breast cancer. I give thanks that modern medicine has been able to make great strides in treating breast cancer and **I would encourage all women to use this** *Life Saving* **device.**

HOWEVER, I fail to understand why it is possible for man to be able to look from a satellite buried in space and see an animal deep in the woods on earth, relieving itself, yet no one can invent a machine that can see through a few inches of flesh?!! Now, how many miles up in space is that satellite? A couple of hundred thousand at least wouldn't you say? Now, how big is a woman's breast? Umm, maybe four to five inches for a small one, seven to eight for a large one. (Ok, I'll get the ruler out another time.) Alright, let's finish this calculation. I believe the ratio of seven to eight inches of flesh to a couple of hundred thousand miles should be a doable comparison. So if you can design a telescope that allows you to see a couple hundred thousand miles, don't you think **Somebody** should be able to design one that can see through a few inches of flesh! I don't believe my logic and rationale is very flawed here!!! I'm sure if men had to have one of their particularly sensitive body parts examined with this device on a yearly basis, somebody would be motivated to re-design that machine quick, fast and in a double-duty hurry!

In the mean time, here is my want ad:

"**WANTED:** One **Female** engineer capable of designing a mammogram machine that will not squeeze the life and feeling out of a breast. The candidate must submit to the MMPI (Minne-

...DNNSMLISE

sota Multiple Personality Inventory.) This inventory is capable of detecting deviant personalities. I do not want to risk having another machine designed by someone who fails to understand that the breast is a very tender thing, with very delicate nerve endings and should be treated gently. I guarantee a substantial fee as well as the eternal gratitude and undying loyalty of women everywhere. Please submit your resume and the number of mammograms to which you have submitted. Multiple mammograms are a **Mandatory** prerequisite, only one who has been through this torture will be able to understand the need for a kinder and gentler machine. Please feel free to contact me day or night. It would be looked upon very favorably if you apply directly after having had a mammogram, that way I'll know the pain is still fresh in your mind. I and millions of women look forward to hearing from you **Immediately**!"

Please, just let me get this new machine up and running and then I promise to find someone to take care of those ice cold intimate devices and gadgets gynecologist seem to love to introduce us to!!

Getting Old

Please, give me a moment to compose myself. I've just had a terrible shock. Perhaps it would be best if I started at the beginning.

I was having lunch with a co-worker, Lanina Cavicchio. She was talking about how active her mother is, traveling and enjoying life. I asked her "How old is your mother?" She said very calmly, "Oh, about your age." Well needless to say I was stunned. I had assumed Lanina and I are close in age. I should have known better than that. (You know what they say about assume, it makes an a-- out of you and me.) Now without revealing her mother's personal business, we are not close in age. Well, it is closer than I'd like to admit.

I'm finding this aging process to be well, different. When my kids try to tell me I'm old (CRS and things like that), I just dismiss them. What child doesn't think their parents are old? So what if I have a few gray hairs, that doesn't make me old. Most of them are coming from me trying to get Jamilah through her teenage years. Lord knows what I'll look like when Askari finishes going through his metamorphosis. Who cares if my kids have to keep me hip to the latest slang terms? So what if they have given up trying to teach me the latest dances as a lost cause? I think they gave up after the Bubble Gum or was it the Flintstones? What do I care, I can still party with the best of them- I think. All kids go through these things with their parents.

But this was different. Here I was getting confirmation from an objective party that the aging process is taking place, whether I want to believe it or not. Somehow, aging seems to be something that takes place with someone else. Yes, I remember saying I'm a prude. I just thought that meant I had a different sense of fashion. I've seen some senior citizen groups perform in dance groups and other venues. I always admire them and their energy level. I've even gone up to some of them and said, "I want to be just like you when I grow up!" I figured I still have some time left before I was that grown up. Another example of this aging process is the time Daveda and I went to the movies and I tried to use my student l.D. card to get a discount. They were only honoring senior citizen discounts. I told her, jokingly of course, pretty soon we'd be able to get that. Hey, I wasn't serious!

I am fortunate to come from the family I do. My parents and grandparents aged gracefully and well. I had an aunt who was doing cartwheels at seventy-five years of age. She, along with one of her sisters, were still traveling all over the world

...DNNSMLISE

when they were well into their sixties. I had another aunt who told me she was traveling down to the Bahamas for a party for the week-end and she was seventy-five. My grandfather married again after all twelve of his children were grown and gone. Can't say I haven't had good examples of how life goes on way past, well let's just say past your twenties. Anything else might give my age way. Maya Angelou has said for years, "a woman is not suppose to tell her age" and I have held to that. At the same time though, I feel like and I do, celebrate each and every year that I have been able to survive and still have my sanity.

But I have to admit, the more I watch some folks grow old, the more I am convinced there has to be a better way. It's like when I was pregnant with Jamilah. In the natural childbirth class, the instructor showed a film of a woman in labor. I already knew how babies got here (obviously) but when you know you are about to enter that process, you pay closer attention to the training film. It wasn't too bad until the baby was being born. They showed how wide the opening gets, how they had to cut the woman to aid in the delivery, and other things I won't mention. I was stunned! I could believe after all these millions of years, somebody couldn't come up with a better way! It's not pretty and it hurts. There I was about to go through that same process in less than two months. Panic began to set in and in one of those rare instances, I was ready to join the crew of blaming men for everything. I finally stopped blaming men and survived the process. I'm not so sure about surviving this aging process.

I have already had some signs that the aging process is no longer on the way but is here. I had been told by my eye doctor that I would need glasses in the future My future is here as I wear glasses now. I probably should have gotten bifocals, instead, I played peek-a-boo, as I have to put my glasses on to read and take them off to see people. I finally broke down and

Don't Need No Soaps, My Life Is Soap Enough!

bought "halfies". Talk about being old! I get unexplained aches in my joints from time to time and of course there's the gray hairs. It's probably because I don't look my age, that I thought I was escaping. It just serves to give me delusions. **HOWEVER**, I refuse to go out without a fight. I managed to get rid of the fat demons on my waist and I eat sensibly to keep them away. Oh alright, yes, I still eat cookies and ice cream. Hey, a girl (gee, I'm beginning to like the sound of that!) has to have some pleasures!

Well, I decided to do something about this aging process. So what do I do? I work out regularly and I stay active. I think that's the real key. If you are doing things and keeping busy, old age has a harder time catching up to you. And I've come to realize how large a part personality plays in all of this. Sweet old ladies weren't born old and sweet, they were born young and sweet. Ornery, cranky old folks weren't born ornery, cranky and old but if that is their personality, old age just seems to make them more ornery and cranky. I found a banner for my last birthday party that has become my motto. It says, "If getting older is better, I'm approaching magnificence!" And I won't buy my bifocals until it's absolutely necessary! Besides, I've got to get busy practicing my cartwheels. Somebody has to keep that family tradition going!

...DNNSMLISE

DNNSMLISE...　Bea Joyner

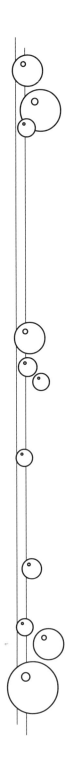

DNNSMLISE...

EPILOGUE

I hope you have enjoyed my "Soaps". I think that some of these chapters would make some Grammy winning blues or country music songs. ("Love Will Make A Hard Behind and A Soft Head" or "Card Carrying Member of the CRS Club".) As I told you I don't need no soaps. With a soap opera, you can stop watching it for six months and when you come back you will still know what is happening. You can't do that with real life. Well, I've got too many things to do to be that involved in someone else's life who isn't real and has no connection with me. Sorry T.V. executives, this is one female who is too busy living her own life to watch your stories. But I'm available if you run out of ideas!

...DNNSMLISE

DNNSMLISE...   Bea Joyner

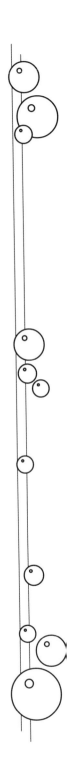

DNNSMLISE...

Don't Need No Soaps, My Life Is Soap Enough!

...DNNSMLISE

ORDER FORM

Telephone orders: (215) 871-0937
Postal Orders: Busy As A Bea Productions
              PO Box 40716-01
              Philadelphia, PA 19107

Please send _____ copies of:
Don't Need No Soaps, My Life Is Soap Enough
              @ $12.95 USA/$17.95 Canada

Subtotal _____
Sales Tax_____
(Please add 7% Pennsylvania
Shipping and Handling)_____
Total $_____

Payment: money orders or checks only

Please ship the book(s) to:

Name: _____

Address: _____

City: _____

State: _____

Zip Code: _____

Telephone: (   ) _____